TEMPORARY SHEPHERDS:

A Congregational Handbook for Interim Ministry

ROGER S. NICHOLSON, EDITOR

An Alban Institute Book
ROWMAN & LITTLEFIELD
Lanham • Boulder • New York • Toronto • Plymouth, UK

First Rowman & Littlefield paperback edition 2014

Published by Rowman & Littlefield
4501 Forbes Blvd, Suite 200, Lanham, MD 20706
www.rowman.com

10 Thornbury Road
Plymouth PL6 7PP
United Kingdom

Library of Congress Cataloging-in-Publication Data Available

ISBN 13: 978-1-56699-208-4 (pbk   )

Printed in the United States of America

CONTENTS

FOREWORD

For everything there is a season. Indeed, a handbook that addresses a congregation's need for intentional interim ministry is truly in season. Not only is the handbook timely, but it is also tested, having been written by a group of experienced, interim ministers. Their collective wisdom offers a comprehensive and panoramic view of what interim ministry can provide for a congregation.

I have advocated this ministry strongly and publicly, especially because I view the local church to be a system. When a pastor leaves by retirement, resignation, reassignment, or the acceptance of a call, the departure changes the system. Transitions disrupt patterns. A hallmark of a system is that change in one part affects all the other parts. There can be a variety of responses to the cleric's exit—fear, anger, confusion, maybe even relief. At any rate, the whole system is suddenly quite different. Special attention is needed, and this attention is precisely what the intentional interim minister offers.

When pastoral leadership changes, the congregation becomes an open system. It is in a position to learn more about itself and its future, but it must be willing and ready to do so. Trained interim pastors are integral to that process of learning. They have been equipped to lead the journey of discovery and planning. Most systems, however, once they become open, want to return to their former state as soon as possible. "Why wait?" asks the congregation, thereby closing the system prematurely. This handbook addresses that almost universal instinct. It recognizes the impulse to put the system back into a steady state. Interim ministry is an acknowledgment that keeping the system open for learning supersedes the instinct for returning to the old, balanced form of doing things. In the meantime, there will be significant lessons for congregations, lessons known as the developmental tasks.

This handbook will direct you to the pertinent topics and processes you will work through during a transitional period. It will help you to minimize mistakes. And it will certainly assist you in preparing for your future with insight, resources, and hope. The book is timely, tested, and a tribute to the value of learning at a critical moment in the congregation's life. More importantly, the book will keep you centered on mission and ministry, the very purpose of any congregation's existence. Interim ministers may be "temporary shepherds," but they can have meaningful, long-term effects on the lives of congregations.

Peter L. Steinke
Author of *How Your Church Family Works* and *Healthy Congregations*

PREFACE

When the Alban Institute approached me regarding authoring a book about interim ministry for use in congregations, I was at first a bit daunted. Such a volume, it seemed to me, could not be the work of one writer. Interim ministry, as we know it today, has evolved over more than two decades, as clergy and laity have learned what it means for a congregation to be between installed pastors. Great impetus for this specialized parish ministry came from the seminal writings of William Yon, Loren Mead, Alan Macy, and others under the auspices of the Alban Institute. Indeed, it would be difficult to list all who have informed interim ministry as a highly specialized field of leadership in parish ministry. Each denomination has had its architects, people such as Alan Gripe, Jill Hudson, and Joan Mabon of the Presbyterian Church; Jim Davis of the Evangelical Lutheran Church; Leigh Early, Terry Foland, Clark Hargus, and Nancy Tanner of the Christian Church, Disciples of Christ; Roy Coffin and Philip Porcher of the Episcopal Church; Char Burch, Dan Hatch, and Robert Stevens of the United Church of Christ; or Kenneth Blazier, Cathleen Narowitz, and Howard Washburn of the American Baptist Church.

As I thought about the project, it became clear to me that a book about interim ministry really would be best authored by people who are actually serving as interim pastors. Who better to give congregations the flavor of ministry during transition than those who serve as pastoral leaders during "in-between times"? Thus my response to the Alban Institute was that I would be willing to edit such a book and seek to bring together contributions from women and men whose daily lives are immersed in interim ministry—people who have served a variety of churches in several denominations and also denominational staff members who have been deeply involved in overseeing this specialty for their denominations. This book is, then, a symposium of stories about interim ministry and a compilation, by no means exhaustive, of resources that have been found to be helpful.

My first attempt at being editor of a book has been challenging and enjoyable. Out of the host of talented people who certainly could have contributed to this volume, I sought a mix of women and men who represented several denominations. The goal has been to provide a readable and informative resource to help congregations understand and benefit by intentional interim ministry. I have tried as best I can to give credit to sources while recognizing, as those professionals in the field will understand, the highly eclectic nature of the specialty and the difficulty of tracking the origins of ideas which have been so freely shared by the many advocates of intentional interim ministry.

Special recognition should be given to the Interim Ministry Network of Baltimore, Maryland, which through the years has brought together the very best interim pastors, providing a forum for learning and growing. As one of the finest ecumenical professional bodies, the Interim Ministry Network is deeply committed to serving Christ's church through the preparation of church and pastor for effective ministry during times of transition. I cannot overstate how valuable the network has been to me personally as an interim pastor and to my denomination, the United Church of Christ. I am sure my colleagues in other denominations would concur.

I would be remiss if I did not thank the Alban Institute for the opportunity to work on this project and all those in the Interim Ministry Network who have lent encouragement in so many ways. Finally, I express appreciation to my wife Anne for her generous contributions of time and word processing expertise, not to mention her enthusiastic and steady support of my interim career spanning nearly 15 years and involving more than 20 congregations. In the end it was the joy of knowing what good things interim ministry accomplished in those 20 congregations which compelled me to accept this opportunity of preparing a handbook for congregations about the in-between times.

Roger S. Nicholson

INTRODUCTION

Roger S. Nicholson

The Changing Church

When I was ordained a parish minister in 1952, churchgoing was a burgeoning post-World War II American pastime. People were flocking to the churches of the land. "Religion in American Life" billboards dotted the landscape. New sanctuaries and parish houses were being erected everywhere. The first Easter after being called to a pastorate in Connecticut, our congregation received 62 new members. The setting of that church was typical for that decade—a new church erected on former farmland which was now surrounded by housing subdivisions. Typical also was the fact that the congregation had been planted by the denomination, which had drawn upon its considerable resources to get the parish started. The congregation grew and became self-supporting, able to contribute its fair share to the denomination's mission. Now, 45 years later and in retirement, I visit and preach around that same conference and find myself wondering, "Where have all the people gone?"

Mainline Protestant denominations have been in a steady decline for nearly a generation. In contrast to receiving a new member group of 62 people, most pastors today rejoice if they are able to welcome a half dozen new members, and more often than not, these new members are apt to be transfers from other churches, not new recruits professing faith for the first time. In addition, denominations that once busied themselves with church expansion now find themselves downsizing as resources steadily diminish. Profound sociological and cultural changes have occurred in America since the halcyon days of the 1950s and have caused a large-scale abandonment of the institutional church by an entire generation. Thousands of local churches struggle to remain viable in the midst of a rapidly changing society. The parish church which greeted me upon graduation from seminary in 1952 is a far different place as the twentieth century nears its end, and what the parish church of the new century will be is not yet clear.

On a recent late-night flight back to Connecticut from a conference in the Midwest, it was made painfully clear to me how the societal context of the local church has changed. The seat next to me was occupied by a young woman attorney returning from an errand for her Hartford law firm. She inquired about my vocation and the reason I was traveling. Upon learning that I was an interim minister, she seemed interested in hearing more about why there was a need for such a specialty. I replied that it would help me to answer her question if I had some idea of her acquaintance with congregational life. She told me that she had been christened as a child—Congregational, she thought—but her family had never been active in any church. Her family always went away on weekends, skiing in the winter and to the beaches in the summer. Her experience of churches was mainly from attending weddings and funerals through the years. Now married, she and her husband enjoyed an active social life on weekends with many cultural and recreational pursuits. As the jet was coming in to land, our conversation ended with her words, "To be honest with you, we have never felt the need of going to church, even though we both do believe in God." Driving home from the airport that night, I realized that I had experienced an encounter with a representative of the legions of young adults in America upon whom the church has no claim and little if any influence. They are not against the church, just indifferent to it.

I have shared this personal story with you because it seems to me to sum up a lot of what has happened to the local church. Basically, it would appear that we have lost an entire generation to what Tony Campolo, a Christian sociologist, refers to in his insightful book *Can Mainline Denominations Make a Comeback?* as the "culture war."[1] Like the young attorney on the flight home, many of her generation certainly believe themselves to be Christians, but they never go to church on Sunday. Although they have decent moral values, they are hard-pressed to define their faith in the midst of a diverse and pluralistic society. Further, the leisure revolution, now so strongly entrenched in American culture, has reduced church affiliation to a very low priority for most young adults. The phenomenon has a long and complex history. Beginning in the 1960s there has been a steady erosion of commitment to religious institutions resulting in what some refer to as "the graying of the local church." The older generation decreases steadily by attrition while the younger generation goes its own way, with little or no sense of responsibility for the church of their baptism. This is more than a little dismaying for those of us who have labored mightily for the local church through our careers, but we are heartened by the thinking of futurist theologians like Loren Mead, whose stimulating book *The Once and Future Church* provides helpful perspective and gives hope for the future.[2]

Bewildered though we may be by the way things are changing, we are not without faith that God is re-shaping the church in ways we cannot yet see. A new form of the local church may already be emerging out of the yet powerful and creative bodies of Christ's people we know today. It is our faith that the church is God's creation, and what God means it to be in the future will be made plain. Speaking through the prophet Isaiah, God says, "Behold, I am doing a new thing; now it springs forth, do you not perceive it?" (Isa. 43:19, RSV)

As a garden-variety pastor who has loved and worked for the local church for more than four decades, I see five realities that make pastoral ministry more challenging and difficult today than it has ever been. These understandings come out of 46 years of active parish ministry. They reflect consultations with church leaders of many traditions, and extensive reading of analyses and critiques by many of the church's best critics—leaders and scholars who are themselves part of the church. These realities come to bear upon congregational life in stressful ways, leading to clergy burnout, shorter-term pastorates, and all too often destructive congregational conflict. They are the context out of which the need for intentional interim ministry has emerged.

Resistance to Change

The first reality is institutional resistance to change. Congregations need to change the way they do things if they are to reach and hold onto the new generations. This is especially true about worship styles. For example, music and language of the nineteenth century no longer attract the young adults of the 1990s. The introduction of new worship resources, such as hymnals with inclusive or gender-neutral language, will be controversial for many congregations, as will the use of livelier music. It is clearly around such basic issues of change that congregational stress and conflict develop. As local churches struggle to find the new approaches they must take to be effective in the new millennium, it is the careful management of change that will be crucial. There is much intense debate about this sort of change in the mainline churches today. Some see it as a lowering of standards and quality; others see it as a strategy of growth and outreach. The challenge is one of discovering new ways of communicating the timeless message of the Gospel in an increasingly secular and materialistic culture. As the twentieth century ends, local congregations struggle with questions bearing upon their very survival. It is not just a simple matter of tinkering with the machinery of congregational life. What is happening may well be being foreshadowed by the experience of congregations in Great Britain. Andrew Rook, a United Reformed Church lay leader in England, recently wrote to his fellow members words strikingly pertinent, even prophetic, for mainline American churches:

> If our only vision of the future of our church harks back to a golden era in our past, then we are doing ourselves no favors in trying to plan for that future. The reality of those days will not return. We live in a new world that is becoming driven by constant activity and by increasingly sophisticated systems of communication and leisure activity, and we have to find and assert our new place in this world. We have to grasp hold of reality in working out where the United Reformed Church as a denomination is going. The number of members and the number of ministers are both decreasing at a steady and predictable rate. These changes tell us the future: a world of pagan assumptions, with little or no knowledge or understanding of Christianity, and no respect for Christian ethics, traditions or institutions, where Christian teaching will be scorned by many; a world that would be recognized by Paul and the other leaders of the early Church in the eastern Mediterranean countries. We are a remnant. We are a small minority, marginalized by society. Do not be afraid of this. If we have a faith that is vital, we need to express it and live it out in a way that firstly recognizes this marginalization, and secondly asserts that we are a church of—and for—people and faith.[3]

Redefining Purpose and Mission

The second reality is the need to redefine purpose and mission in the modern settings of the church. The biblical warning, "Where there is no vision the people perish" (Prov. 29:18, KJV), has never been more apt than it is today. Clarity about theological foundations, doctrine, and social mission is critical in our modern pluralistic world if congregations are to have a clear sense of identity and direction. Yet we all know it is precisely in these areas that differences of opinion can cause considerable strife. One of the most challenging things a congregation may be called upon to do is to define itself theologically, or to explain the congregation's understanding of the Bible. In my work as an area representative of my denomination I frequently found myself being called upon to referee contests between church members who were at different places in regard to the interpretation of Scripture. Most mainline congregations are made up of members who are at varying points on the conservative-liberal spectrum regarding scripture and theology. The potential for strong disagreement and congregational turmoil is always present. Sensitive and skilled leadership is increasingly essential to help congregations with self-study and redefinition of their mission to the community and world of which they are a part.

The Need for Viable Stewardship

The third reality is the challenge to exercise viable Christian stewardship. I write this fresh from a meeting at the church I belong to during which the proposed operating budget was not approved because it was a deficit budget. The pledging of members had fallen woefully short of what was needed. Graphs prepared by the finance committee showed a trend in which congregational expenses continued to exceed income from member giving, despite the strong efforts of the stewardship committee. A sense of gloom filled the room. Some proposed the reduction of mission giving and denominational support. Diminishing financial support to mainline Protestant churches is common across the nation. Lack of both relevance and a sense of purpose underlies the inadequate stewardship so widespread in churches today. Some say there are too many churches maintaining too many expensive buildings, siphoning off resources needed for outreach; others insist it is more a matter of teaching and training believers to give the way they should. However the crisis may be expressed, it seems clear that Christian stewardship is a crucial arena for effective leadership in the emerging congregations of the second millennium.

Local church stewardship is significantly impacted by the congregation's relationship to its denomination. There has been a marked turning away from denominational mission giving in favor of more parochial outreach. Local churches increasingly channel their giving toward local needs. National mission boards, created by local congregations to reach out to the world on their behalf, more often find themselves having to justify their existence. Much tension and conflict cluster around issues relating to the allocation of scarce resources. As giving decreases, programs begin to decline, congregations reduce staff, and a downward cycle accelerates toward a survival mentality. Stress develops between clergy leadership and the laity. Conflict emerges, pastors leave, and transition periods increase in frequency.

Controversial Social Issues

A fourth reality of the modern predicament of the local church is that controversial social issues will continue to produce conflict and tension well into the future for mainline denominations. Two major debates—the questions of sexual preference and abortion—will be center stage, but other issues will demand attention as well, including racism, societal violence, separation of church and state, and the increasing pressure on religious organizations brought about by the diminishing role of government in social services. As congregations struggle with issues of justice and peace, differences of opinion will strain relationships among members and between members and pastors. Management of these connections will require sensitive and skilled leadership. There has always been tension in churches between those who would separate church life from social issues and those who insist that the church belongs in the forefront of the quest for a just and equitable society. The emergence in the 1980s and 1990s of the highly politicized "religious right" signals the continuation and intensification of an atmosphere of confrontation around social issues unlike anything mainline congregations have contended with in the past. For the foreseeable future this will be a reality impacting local church life and ministry.

Increasing Diversity

A fifth reality facing the local church is the increasing diversity in American society with a consequent blurring of differences in religious traditions. There is rising opinion that the day of denominationalism is past, and the sooner Christians consolidate their resources and influence, the better it will be for all churches. Recent accords among several mainline traditions at denominational levels need to be consummated on the local level. Ultimately there may well be mergers of local parishes of different traditions, but such an eventuality will not be without pain and resistance when the time comes, say, to actually close buildings. Exciting possibilities lie ahead for church unity, but these possibilities will not be accomplished without vision and commitment to change. The approaching new century brings with it the question of whether local congregations will be able to give up their parochial, traditional, edifice-oriented ways to further a new, more ecumenical and less competitive model of the church.

Given this context, the time is right for the emergence of a new specialty in church leadership—intentional interim ministry. To this we now turn our attention.

Intentional Interim Ministry

Sooner or later every congregation will experience the loss of a pastor. However, in the midst of all the complex cultural and societal change affecting congregations today, the end of many pastoral relationships appears to be happening sooner more often than later. The incidence of conflict in congregations is increasing. There is a disturbing increase in incidents of ministerial misconduct. Pastorates are tending to be shorter in duration. More and more congregations find themselves in transition, not only in terms of contextual change, but also in terms of leadership. Although it is true that pastoral changes have taken place for generations, it is only in recent years that the period which ensues at the departure of an installed pastor has been recognized as a time of unique importance in a congregation's life. A shift in emphasis has occurred. Although at one time church leaders saw the period of a pastoral vacancy as a maintenance task—keeping things going, providing for the supply of the pulpit and pastoral emergencies, and finding a replacement pastor as quickly as possible—now more and more informed church leaders see the time as an opportunity to do much more than just keep the parish wheels turning. A process has been developed which enhances the congregation's future health and progress. The process is intentional interim ministry.

Intentional interim ministry is a studied response to the unique need and opportunity that a change of pastors brings. However, congregations need help in understanding both the dynamics of the interim period and the role of the interim leader if they are to make the most of the transition at hand. Questions always arise when a pastoral vacancy occurs: "Why do we need interim ministry? Why can't we just arrange for supply of the pulpit and get on with finding a new pastor as quickly as possible?" By way of beginning to answer such understandable questions, let me share with you three vignettes from my recent experience as a denominational liaison minister to churches about to enter transition:

1. The five members of the executive committee of First Church listened quietly to my presentation about the long process they were beginning now that their pastor of 26 years was retiring. I had been invited to come and advise them about what to do to obtain a new pastor. I sensed their impatience and discomfort as I detailed the process which could require several months, if not a year or longer.

"That's ridiculous!" said a young executive of a local corporation. "My company would have a replacement in six weeks. We should just get out there and hire someone immediately. Let's not waste time."

Heads nodded. I took a deep breath and . . .

2. "We really don't have a problem," said a deacon of West Side Church as the council began discussion about the surprise resignation of their senior minister. "Let's just ask our wonderful associate minister to step up and take over. Everyone loves her, and it will save the bother of a long search. That way we won't lose any ground."

Even though I had come to the meeting as the denomination's spokesperson, ready to offer them resources and support for their leadership transition, I was not entirely surprised by this not-so-hidden agenda. As heads nodded, I took a deep breath and . . .

3. The moderator and senior elder from Union Church seemed rather down as we shared a cup of coffee in my office at the conference center.

"Here we go again," the elder began. "Reverend Douglas's resignation could have been expected. We've had three ministers now in less than 10 years. None stays. What's wrong with us anyway? I doubt we'll get a new one, and if we do, we won't keep him."

The moderator nodded. I took a deep breath and . . .

There is nothing so disconcerting for a congregation as a change of pastors. Whatever the circumstances, the departure of a spiritual leader always brings dismay to a faith community, stirring a mixture of strong feelings and presenting a time of anxious uncertainty and even a sense of confusion. As in vignettes one and two above, there may be a rush to find a quick fix or, as in the third vignette, there may be a mood bordering on despair, reflecting a congregation's poor self-image. Pastoral changes bring with them a wide spectrum of reactions and feelings. The time between installed pastors—the interim time—is always a time of crucial significance to a congregation. Just as nature abhors a vacuum and rushes to fill it, so it would seem a congregation abhors a pastoral vacancy and seeks to fill it as quickly as possible. Members wonder who will baptize the children, marry the young couples, counsel the troubled, preside over rites of burial, or minister to the suffering, the bereaved, and the lonely. What will become of the church's programs and ministries? Will there be erosion of membership and financial giving?

Less tangible, but possibly more significant than such day-to-day concerns about parish life, are the deeper emotional dimensions of separation and change in individual members and in the corporate body. There is no bond quite like the bond that develops between people and pastor. Feelings of grief, a sense of loss and abandonment, anger and disappointment, confusion and uncertainty—all of these emotions typically arise when an admired and beloved leader departs, and if there has been misunderstanding or conflict in the congregation's life, there will also be resentment and guilt in the mix. Alban Institute research has

shown that rushing out and getting a new pastor as quickly as possible is
a risky business. When a pastoral change occurs, a unique opportunity is
at hand for the congregation. Loren Mead, Alban Institute's former president, calls this opportunity "a critical moment of ministry."[4]

When a change of pastors occurs, a congregation needs time to ad-
just. This may well take the form of grieving for a beloved friend who
has moved on, or it may be a time of resolving bad feelings left over
from conflict and misunderstanding. What is needed is a chance to get
perspective on a relationship that has ended. Emotional adjustments do
not respect timetables. The pressures of schedules ought not be allowed
to stifle healthy emotional expression. At the same time, however, there
is basic work to be done to get ready for a new leader, work that can go
forward as emotional adjustment runs its necessary course. Indeed, creative attention to the work of the interim time can help people to come
to terms with their feelings. As the congregation begins to take stock of
itself, to assess its strengths and weaknesses, and to refocus its sense of
identity and mission, new understanding of the past emerges, along with
an increasing readiness to move forward in new ways with a new leader.

This is a book about the time between pastors, the interim time.
There's a journey awaiting the interim congregation and there are skilled
pastors available to lead this journey—women and men who are intentional interim ministers called to a specialized work with congregations
in transition. Many are members of the Interim Ministry Network, an
ecumenical body that trains interim church leaders to help congregations
make the most of the interim opportunity.[5] This book, to which many
intentional interim ministers have contributed out of their experience
leading the interim journey with congregations, is a guidebook for the
journey. It is a pooling and sharing of knowledge about the interim time,
with practical suggestions and proven approaches for congregations facing into change. Less than two decades ago there were few aids to congregations entering the interim time. Now much has been learned and it
is time to share the experience and help congregations move toward the
future purposefully and creatively, benefiting from the journeys of
others. Those of us who have contributed to this volume hope that you
will enjoy the journey. It will be exciting and fulfilling, but not without
risk and challenge. It can be fun, and we hope very much that this will
be the case for your congregation. Above all, we hope that the interim
journey will result in a healthier, happier, and more faithful people of
God in your community.

PART 1

The Interim Congregation

CHAPTER 1

The Challenge of the Interim Time

Roger S. Nicholson

It's a familiar and humorous story, the anecdote about the big city sales-man who got lost in Vermont. Driving along a backcountry road, he came upon a farmer getting his mail at the end of the driveway which led up to the farmhouse.

"Excuse me, sir," said the weary salesman. "Could you please tell me where I am?"

"Yep," came the reply. "You're in Gallup's Mills."

With a sigh the frustrated salesman asked, "Well, could you kindly direct me to Lyndonville?"

Pondering for a moment, the farmer replied, "You can't get there from here."

Anyone who has ever been lost in strange territory can empathize with the salesman, and although we may chuckle at the stereotypical farmer, upon reflection we can see that very often in life, where we start from can have a great deal to do with where we end up and how we get there. Quite probably the farmer did go on to say something like, "Well, stranger, you need to go back a few miles and take a different turn, and you'll get there all right." Let us at least give him the benefit of the doubt. In my experience Vermont folks are really very kind and helpful people.

A congregation facing that time between the end of one pastorate and the beginning of another is entering strange territory. This time between installed pastors is known in churches as the interim time. It is not unlike driving down a road you have never traversed before. It has been likened to the biblical time of wandering in the wilderness after the flight of the Hebrew people from Egypt. A sense of lostness, confu-sion, and uncertainty may be present in the congregation. There may be pronounced anxiety about the future that prevents people from focusing on the present. As with those ancient Hebrews in the Sinai desert, there may be murmuring and complaining when routines get upset and when accustomed services and programs are disrupted or changed. It is not unusual for there to be wounds left from angry disagreements between the departed pastor and groups of members, and there may be hard feelings that prevent people from looking forward to better days. If there has been malfeasance, such as unethical conduct by a pastor, there will be a mood of betrayal and mistrust clouding the atmosphere of congregational life.

How does a people of faith, a religious community, find its way through such thickets of feelings? How does a worshipping fellowship come to grips with its sense of self and its reason for being? How can it get "there" from "here"—from the closing of one significant chapter in its life to the opening of the next, coming with wholeness and harmony to the threshold of its future? The testimony of many congregations who have taken the interim road is that you *can* get there from here. There is a map for the journey, one that has been used successfully by many congregations and interim leaders. There are people to guide the congregation on this journey, pastors specifically trained to help congregations through the wilderness of change. To speak of "there" in the context of a church that is between installed pastors is to speak of the congregation coming to a state of readiness to greet a new leader and begin a new period of worship and ministry, unhindered by unresolved problems of the past and inspired by a new understanding of its mission. When we speak of "here" in the context of the interim time, we are speaking of the overall condition of the congregation at the start of the interim journey. This may encompass many areas: the feeling life of its members; the state of its stewardship; the social context in which it finds itself; what is happening to attendance and membership growth; and what its strengths and weaknesses are. These are all vital signs of the congregation's life.

The map of the journey mentioned above began to take shape in 1974 when the Alban Institute, a highly respected, church-related research organization in Washington, D.C., published the findings of studies about the interim time in congregations. These studies had been prompted by the increasing amount of conflict in churches and by the question of why new pastorates that followed ones which had ended in conflict, or ones where the incumbent had died in office, or ones where there had been a long and happy relationship between people and pastor, tended to be short pastorates which too often ended on a less than harmonious note. The interim ministry movement owes much to church leaders like Ralph Macy, Loren Mead, and William Yon for seminal writings which undergird present understandings of the interim period in congregations. Macy's *The Interim Pastor*, Mead's *The Developmental Tasks of a Congregation in Search of a Pastor*, and Yon's *Prime Time for Renewal* are basic reading for leaders of interim congregations, both lay and clergy. These important works are listed in the bibliography at the end of this book.

Getting Our Bearings

Those who have explored the period between settled pastors in congregations have provided a framework for intentional interim ministry called stages and tasks. Congregations experience eight stages in the interim journey. The journey begins with *termination*. This is the stage marked by the departure of the incumbent pastor. It concerns the closure of a chapter in the congregation's life that began when the person who is leaving was called. It is a time of farewell, with all the accompanying emotions of separation and uncertainty.

The end of the pastorate impels the congregation to the second stage of the journey, *direction finding*. This is a time of learning about the steps to be taken before a new pastor will be called. Consultation with denominational leaders will outline the process and help secure interim leadership for the journey. The purpose of direction finding is to reduce anxiety and reassure the congregation that all will be well.

Once an interim pastor is on hand and has taken hold of things, the congregation begins the third stage of the journey, which is *self-study*. This should be an unhurried process of the congregation looking at itself, gathering data, and preparing a parish description to share with prospective candidates. It is a careful and deliberate process of evaluation.

The fourth stage in the journey is the actual *search* for the new pastor, which cannot begin until the congregation has clearly focused its identity. The search stage requires intensive work by the search committee.

Usually it follows denominational procedures. Many candidate profiles will be studied, culminating in interviews of a few candidates. The search stage is encased in strict confidentiality, and there is very often an air of secrecy abroad in the congregation. It is a time of increasing anticipation, but also of impatience, requiring the search committee to keep in touch with the congregation on a regular basis.

Stage five in the journey is called *decision*. This is the exciting climax of the search when a candidate is presented and the congregation decides whether or not to extend a call. Decision leads quickly into stage six, *negotiation*, during which the appropriate church leaders finalize the details of salary, benefits, and starting date for the new pastor, and a covenant or contract is agreed upon.

Stage seven of the interim journey is the *installation* of the new pastor, a stage which may vary in length. Stage eight is known as *start-up*. It is the official beginning of a new pastorate and of a new chapter in the congregation's life.

As the congregation progresses through the stages of the interim journey, it undertakes the developmental tasks, guided and encouraged by an intentional interim pastor. Let us now briefly consider these five tasks.

The Developmental Tasks

Task 1: Coming to Terms with History

One of the essentials for a congregation facing the uncertainties that a change of pastors brings is to get perspective on itself, to come to an appreciation of where it is as a corporate body—emotionally, spiritually, historically, and sociologically. A congregation needs to do this intentionally, to step back, as it were, and take a long, unhurried look at it-self. I remember an experience when I was hiking one day over a 30-mile stretch of Vermont's Long Trail through the wonderful Green Mountains. We had been hiking for several hours and it was time to rest and have a bite to eat. We came upon the perfect spot to set down our packs and catch our breath, a lookout point with a panoramic view. From this vantage point we could look back whence we had come, now several miles in the distance. We could also look out across a beautiful valley 2,000 feet below us, as well as toward our destination to the north where the massive peak of Camel's Hump beckoned. It was a moment which we would always remember—appreciating where we had been, enjoying where we were, and anticipating where we were going.

The interim journey affords a congregation an opportunity not unlike that experience we had on the Long Trail. The interim time is a moment in the congregation's life when the members have a chance to look back and appreciate their history, both recent and long-term; it is also a moment to consider the present scene, discerning the good and the not so good in the congregation's life; and it is a very special opportunity to look ahead and chart out the future course of the congregation. Every change of pastoral leadership is a unique opportunity for a local congregation to learn from its past, weigh its strengths and weaknesses, and prepare itself for a new future under the guidance of a new pastor.

The interim time is probably the most challenging time a congregation may face. In addition to the ongoing need to continue pastoral ministry, to provide for the worship of God and the proclamation of the Gospel, and to attend to the customary agenda of the local parish, there is the crucial transition to be accomplished. Many issues present themselves at a change of pastors. How well these issues are addressed will significantly impact the next installed pastorate and will determine how well the congregation progresses toward furthering its vision for the future.

After its installed pastor has left, a congregation needs to work through its recent experience without losing sight of its longer story. Members need to complete closure with the departed leader, taking time to express their feelings of loss, separation, hurt, disappointment, anger, guilt, or whatever strong emotions may be left over from the ending of the pastoral relationship. This process will be the more complicated to the degree that the separation of people and pastor was the result of conflict that led to an involuntary departure of the leader. The resolution of such dynamics will greatly impact the congregation's readiness to accept a new leader. Painful experience in many congregations has shown that unless conflict is resolved and healthy communication restored prior to the call of a new pastor, the chances for the success of the new pastorate are substantially reduced. Also, a candidate for such a situation is generally wary of giving it serious consideration if she or he senses that the congregation is not harmonious. But conflict is not the only aspect of a congregation's recent past that needs to be given serious attention. Members need time to assess what has been accomplished during the tenure of their departed leader and to discover the strengths and weaknesses of their faith community. It's time to take an unhurried look in the mirror!

Important as it is for the interim congregation to get perspective on the most recent chapter in its life, the longer-term story must not be overlooked. Every congregation has a story to tell about its beginnings, its achievements through the years, its trials, its struggles, and its contributions to the community and the wider Christian world. It is almost always exciting and healing for a faith community to rediscover its past and learn how that past informs the present life of the congregation. I remember pastoring one interim congregation with a rather poor self-image. There was a mood that clearly said, "No one would want to serve this church. What do we have to offer?" I persuaded the interim steering committee to plan a heritage Sunday, a day for the congregation to hear its long story through historical anecdotes and exhibits of memorabilia. Much research was done and amazing things were learned, including the fact that the congregation had sent six missionaries to the western frontier in the nineteenth century. This was the beginning of a new spirit of outreach in a fellowship that had become ingrown and lacking in a sense of purpose beyond its own survival. Getting in touch with its history is a good place for the interim congregation to start.

Task 2: Discovering a New Identity

In a rapidly changing world, many congregations unconsciously think of themselves as not changing. For church folk it is not a very long reach from the conviction that the church's faith and witness is unchanging to the subtle persuasion that the church, as an institution to which they belong, is staying the same. For hosts of people, church is a place where there is stability, familiarity, and security in a world where, as the old deacon in the play *Green Pastures* by Marc Connelly put it, "Everything nailed down is bustin' loose!"

Congregations tend to think that they do not change over time, but nothing is further from the truth. Congregations change significantly as they respond to different pastoral leaders, to changes in their societal context, and to alterations in their internal circumstances. I remember a suburban congregation that still thought of itself as it was in the 1950s when housing subdivisions were going up around it almost overnight and young families were flocking to its doors. "Why, hardly a month went by that we didn't receive new members!" an older lady said during the interview to discuss their interim situation. It was sobering for the group to recognize that during the previous 10 years they had lost many more members than they had received. Their beautiful educational building, which once buzzed with crowds of children, now housed a church school with fewer than 50 students.

The time between installed pastors brings a unique chance for a congregation to come to a new understanding of itself. A self-study process can help focus a congregation's identity, resulting in a picture based on reality and not on fond remembrances of past experience. Much has been learned about how congregations can assess themselves and plan for the future during the interim period. This is basic work which needs to be done before a new pastor is considered so that the search committee which enters into conversations with candidates can accurately describe the congregation and its vision for the future. It has been the experience of scores of churches that discovering a new identity is a process that energizes the congregation, enhances the healing process, and builds excitement and anticipation for the future.

Task 3: Leadership Changes during an Interim

Myron, the chairperson of the search committee for St. John's Parish, was frustrated. For weeks he had been trying to get financial data from Julia, the church treasurer. She had been the treasurer for more years than most members could recall, having taken over the position at the death of her husband who had been the treasurer for many years before. There had always been difficulty getting information from Julia. Reports were infrequent and detail limited. Church leaders, however, did not want to change treasurers, fearing it would create a bad reaction among many long-term members who were close to Julia. There was talk in the congregation that Pastor Langdon had left because he got tired of getting his salary checks late, and there had been a problem with the denomination's pension board regarding late payment of premiums. It was clearly time for a change. Myron sought the advice of the interim pastor. A group of three church officers and the interim pastor met with Julia. To everyone's amazement, she was relieved to have the question of her tenure raised! She had wanted to give up the post for some time, but felt that no one else wanted the job. She was more than ready to take a sabbatical.

It is not unusual for a change in pastoral leadership to bring about changes in the lay leadership of a congregation as well. Sometimes extensive structural changes need to be made in the congregation's way of doing things. One interim pastor discovered that all matters pertaining to church benevolence were being handled by the pastor. Lay people had no say in the outreach giving of the congregation. A process began which led to the establishment of the first committee on mission and outreach in that church's history. Most pastors develop a cadre of supportive lay leaders during their tenure. This is a normal phenomenon in human groups, much like choosing sides to play a game of baseball. Who's going to score the most runs? We need her or him on our side! One of the problems is that this approach can lead to burnout among many leaders of churches. Thus, a change at the top, as it were, may well have a kind of ripple effect as some overworked leaders decide to take time out. One interim pastor was told quite bluntly by an active lay leader that when the previous pastor left the church, he lost interest in serving on the church council. He was doing so only because of his friendship and admiration for the previous minister.

Frequently, a change of pastors provides a chance for new people to step forward into leadership roles. In happier, healthier congregations these shifts of leadership go relatively smoothly as some members retire from responsibility and others are invited to take over. But in conflicted and struggling congregations, such adjustments of leadership may well become power struggles. In these situations skillful management of change is crucial. One of the most difficult characteristics of many congregations is the struggle between generations for leadership control, what some refer to as the old guard versus the newcomers. I remember meeting Greg at the supermarket, not having seen my former neighbor since he moved to a nearby community and joined a small congregation. I asked about his new church and he said, "Oh, we've left there and gone to the church at the center of town. They wouldn't let us younger people have any say about things." I remembered Greg's energetic leadership in the past, and I felt disappointment both for him and for the church. The time between pastors provides a congregation with the opportunity to honestly and lovingly confront such a picture of itself and hopefully bring about needed changes.

Task 4: Renewing Denominational Linkages

It has been the experience of church leaders that congregations in the interim time are more open to cooperation with their denomination than they may have been for a long time, or will be again for a considerable time. Clearly, the time between installed pastors is a special opportunity for both local church and denomination to renew their relationship. Apart from the congregation's need for help in finding a new pastor, there is frequently a quest for denominational identity that comes to the fore during a time of transition. There is more interest in the congregation's origins and traditions. The interim time is a great time for relearning (or learning for the first time) what it means to be a Presbyterian, a Baptist, a Lutheran, an Episcopalian, or a member of the United Church of Christ. The interim time is frequently a time when local church folk discover that denominational bureaucrats are real people. Congregants begin to view church officials as the dedicated and skilled men and women they really are, often for the very first time. Looking into their denominational histories, many local church members are surprised to learn of their church's contributions to the work of Christ through their denomination's wider ministries. One church was amazed to learn that through the years it had sent 16 members into various fields of mission! During the interim time, many denominational resources are available to a congregation in transition. Some denominations provide skilled consultants to guide the congregation through its self-study, or to help manage a difficult conflict situation, or to do long-range planning. All denominations can provide help with leadership training, stewardship development, Christian education resources, and other areas of local church programming. Hosts of congregations have renewed their connections with the wider church during the interim period. More often than not, it becomes a time of discovery and celebration of a rich tradition.

Task 5: Commitment to New Directions in Ministry

As the interim journey progresses, the congregation becomes more ready
to move into the future with a new pastoral leader. Congregational self-
study has clarified the congregation's sense of its uniqueness as a faith
community. Members have become aware of new opportunities for service, while at the same time affirming what is good and well established
in the congregation's life and program. There is an increasing eagerness
to move on and an anticipation for the arrival of a new leader. A readiness for partnership in ministry with the approaching leader emerges. No
longer shackled to its past, the congregation's energy is increasingly
focused on the future. The end of the interim journey is at hand. This is
always a moment of excitement and high expectation. Differences and
misunderstandings have been resolved; closure of the former pastoral
relationship has been completed; a new mission has been discerned; and
members are eager to go forward.

Although there may well be tasks remaining from the interim period, a new spirit of unity will enable these matters to be dealt with, even
as the new pastorate begins. In an open and intentional way, leftover
business will be addressed in cooperation with the new leader. It is rare
for congregations to accomplish everything needing attention during the
interim time. What is important is to attain a condition of harmony, an
atmosphere of readiness to do what is needed in partnership with the
new pastoral leader. An exit interview with the departing interim pastor
and a representative of the denomination will help the lay leadership
clarify what remains to be done so that this information can be shared
early with the new minister.

Ideally, the end of the interim time will be a moment of celebration
of what the journey has accomplished and of the congregation's readiness for a new beginning. Congregations that have conscientiously
pursued the interim tasks will greatly enhance the success of the new
pastorate.

For Reflection and Discussion

1. Discuss the five realities facing congregations today (beginning on page xi in the introduction). How do you see these realities reflected in your congregation? How did they affect your former pastor's ministry?

2. What was your reaction when you learned your pastor was leaving? What reactions have other members shared with you?

3. Reread the three vignettes described on page xvi in the introduction. How do they relate to your church's experience? How did your denominational representative prepare you for your transition?

4. Chapter 1 gives a brief overview of the five developmental tasks of the interim period in congregations. What signs do you see in your church that these tasks are being attended to? What signs do you see that more needs to be done?

5. Change is a part of life. We encounter changes everywhere. How do you feel about change? When is change most difficult for you? Thinking about your church, what seems most important to change? What seems most important to preserve?

CHAPTER 2

Characteristics of the Interim Congregation

Roger S. Nicholson

At a national gathering of interim pastors a few years ago, the question was asked, "Are there similarities among congregations that are between settled or installed pastors? If so, what would a general profile of an interim congregation look like? Or does each interim congregation experience unique issues and dynamics during its time between pastors?"

The shared experience of intentional interim pastors from across North America has yielded a list of characteristics typical of congregations experiencing transition from one pastor to the next. This chapter is about what has been observed in congregations of all denominations and all sizes. Although not every congregation may experience every dynamic, the reader will nevertheless be able to identify those characteristics pertinent to his or her situation. Becoming aware of the issues in a particular setting will help the congregation get ready for a new chapter in its life and ministry. Let us look at ten characteristics typical of the interim congregation through the eyes of real church members.

Grief Will Be Present

Agnes, an active 80-year-old woman, was a lifelong member of North Church, a congregation of 300 members in a college community. As church librarian, she shared a love of books with her pastor for nearly 20 years. She and the pastor's family were very close. She was happy for her pastor when he went away for a study leave, but she was not prepared for what happened upon his return. During his sabbatical he had confirmed his decision to leave North Church. Also, he and his wife had decided to separate. His pastorate had been an exciting and creative one, but had taken its toll. He was leaving the parish ministry for a new career as a corporate consultant. The congregation was shocked and Agnes was devastated, as were many others.

"He was like a son to me," Agnes tearfully told the interim pastor a few weeks later.

When a beloved and admired minister leaves a congregation, there will be a time of grief. Loren Mead has said, "Interim pastors go into a congregation as into a household of grief."[1] Sometimes the sadness and regret is close to the surface, as it was with Agnes. Other times it is masked by feelings of disappointment, anger at abandonment, or a sense of uncertainty and bewilderment. The anxiety level in the congregation is high. There may even be panic expressed by questions such as, "What will become of us now?" There may well be a sense of paralysis and uncertainty marked by a reluctance to make any change or decision. One interim pastor on his very first Sunday was told by a lay official, "Just preach on Sunday, visit the sick, and don't try to change anything. Understand?"

Even the departure of a pastor whose ministry has not been overly successful will be marked by grief. There will always be a portion of the congregation who bonded with the spiritual leader to a deeper extent than others did. Indeed, in such instances members' grief may well be more complicated since it is expressed in anger toward those who are glad at the departure. Members who were fond of the pastor may even believe that others conspired to bring it about. The potential is present in such circumstances for the outbreak of conflict.

For some people the loss of a pastor feels like the loss of a family member. It is not unusual for individuals to experience a resurgence of feelings related to the loss of a parent when faced with the departure of a pastor who has been close to the family. Endings are very often painful. The interim congregation is much like a family contending with endings, with change, and with transition. In an Alban Institute paper shared with interim clergy, Loren Mead writes:

It seems to me that what we're dealing with in transitions . . . all transition, corporate or individual . . . is that we're scared to death to die. We don't want things to change, because any change threatens us with our own end. If we lose our minister, we'll never get the church back to where it was. It's hard to let go of your friends. Every change and every transition is a little death. The fear of death is the ultimate fear. Our anxiety about that ultimate fear makes it hard for us to face into those changes, to grieve and to cry. Our instinct is to retreat, to protect ourselves, not to face into the threat. Parishes want to close off the past and not think about it. As a result, they frequently make disastrous mistakes.[2]

Conflict May Be Latent or Active

Sheldon stopped by the interim minister's office on a Monday morning three weeks into the interim process.

"I just thought you should know," said Sheldon. "Your sermon yesterday about inclusive language and the new hymnal has upset a lot of people, including me. There's no way that hymnal is going to be put in the pew racks of this church!"

The interim pastor soon discovered a simmering controversy in the congregation, conflict between people who wanted change and innovation in worship, and those who did not. He became aware that there were those who felt that the denomination was much too liberal about gender, sexual orientation, and reproductive choice issues. Inclusive language questions were only the tip of an iceberg of controversy.

Interim congregations may frequently experience some level of conflict, ranging from minor problems to armed camps facing each other over life-or-death positions on theological or social questions. Sometimes the conflict is open and visible, but often there is denial that anything is wrong. Whether the conflict is overt or latent, however, there is a preoccupation with it that effectively retards progress toward the congregation's future. Unless the problem is addressed and brought to resolution, the chances for a successful new pastorate are greatly reduced.

Conflict occurs in congregations for all kinds of reasons. Too often the incumbent pastor is the focus of disagreement. It may be as simple as a personality conflict, or as complex as his or her leadership style. Disharmony begins slowly and builds over time, all too frequently ending in open dispute and summary resignation or involuntary termination. The aftermath is a congregation full of hurt feelings and riddled with resentments among members. Skilled management of the situation is the order of the day, and conflicted interim congregations can be healed. A renewed and harmonious fellowship can emerge and indeed must be developed if the congregation is to progress.

Secrets May Be Coming to Light

Janet, the new interim at Olivet Church, at first did not think twice about the insistence of the church's trustees that she post office hours on the church bulletin board. One trustee in particular, Jerry, seemed to be fixated on the subject. Janet noticed, as weeks went by, that he was monitoring her whereabouts. She also became increasingly aware of a vague sense of suspicion about her role from several members. All of this was unspoken, yet intuitively she sensed something was bothering people. Progress seemed slow in the interim tasks and she wondered why.

Several months into the interim, a woman named Beatrice came to see her. Beatrice shared with her the story of how a former pastor had sexually abused her during a counseling session. Bells began to ring in Janet's head. She sensed a pervasive secret in the congregation relating to the ministry of the pastor who had left two short pastorates ago. Gradually Janet unlocked the secret no one in the parish wanted to talk about. Sexual misconduct had indeed occurred and had been hushed up. It had affected two successive, short pastorates. Janet now understood the lack of trust and the attempt by the trustees to unduly control and monitor the activity of the interim in the parish. Janet gently encouraged conversation about the shadowy past, and healing began as feelings were finally shared and the secret opened up. The issue of misconduct was addressed and the perpetrator reported to ecclesiastical authority. The congregation began to move forward again.

Interim congregations often have what might be called hidden agendas, serious issues of the past which have not been resolved. When kept underground, such issues tend to muddy the waters and seriously deter healthy congregational life. In John 8:32 Jesus says, "You will know the truth, and the truth will make you free." In congregational life it is imperative that information be shared by all members. Congregations are remarkable in their ability to resolve problems when all the information about an issue is known by everyone concerned. It is the concealing or avoidance of information that becomes destructive of congregational unity and harmony. The overarching challenge is the preservation of trust among members. When trust is betrayed in misguided attempts by lay leaders to protect congregations, long-term problems of suspicion and doubt usually result. A time of pastoral transition frequently brings such dynamics to the fore. There is an important opportunity at hand for a congregation to be freed of such unhelpful dynamics.

Openness to the Denomination

Arnold looked around the circle of church leaders he had gathered in his living room. "Very good attendance," he thought, as he called the meeting to order. As president of the church council, he was leading the first meeting since the pastor's letter of resignation had been received by the congregation. Arnold had known it was coming, but most members had been taken by surprise. The pastor had decided to take another call after serving St. Mark's for 11 good years. There was general sharing among council members about this—about how good he'd been for the congregation and how hard he'd be to replace.

"We need help, of course," Arnold said. "I've already spoken with the district minister. She wants to come next week to sit down with us and discuss the procedure. How about next Thursday evening at the church?"

Some people had other commitments, but said they would change their plans. The church came first. Arnold was pleased that just about everyone would attend. He was also a little surprised because he knew that many in the parish did not feel much rapport with the denominational office. There had always been resistance to accepting denominational policies and actions, especially requests by the denomination for money. There were some who openly questioned why any connection with the wider church was necessary. Now, here they were, practically embracing a denominational representative!

When a congregation loses its pastor, for whatever reason, it becomes open to outside help in a way that it may not have been for a long time and may not be again for a considerable time. It is a prime opportunity for that congregation to renew its denominational identity and to focus its theological and spiritual traditions. There is a unique readiness to engage the wider church in conversation about common mission and witness. The congregation's need for a new leader is a kind of entry point into a renewed relationship with the denomination, which in significant ways holds the key to the local church's future. The resources of the wider church in Christian education, mission interpretation, leadership development, stewardship growth, and evangelism can be brought to bear more readily and more intentionally upon the congregation's life.

Low Self-Esteem May Prevail

At the supermarket one morning Jeanette met a friend from a neighboring community. They were members of the same denomination, but attended different churches. Jeanette envied her friend's church. It seemed so strong and successful. They were always doing interesting things. She knew that their youth group was about to leave for a week's work camp experience in Appalachia. Jeanette's church didn't even have a youth group, and now her pastor had just resigned to go to a church in the West.

"Here we go again," said Jeanette to her friend. "He's only stayed three years, just like all the others. No one stays long at our church. I guess we just don't have much to offer, really. We may not even get another. I wonder what's wrong with us?"

Not having a ready response, her friend busied herself reading the label on a product.

Many interim congregations, especially smaller ones, have low self-esteem. They can point to few successes in the life of the fellowship. They have not been growing. Visitors are rare. It seems as though it is a constant struggle to make ends meet financially. There is a kind of survival mentality at every business meeting. Nominating committees have great trouble filling all the positions required by the by-laws. Short-term pastorates, in particular, heighten a sense of temporariness about everything. Sometimes there is a reputation abroad that the church is negative and contentious, unwilling to try new things. Membership is ingrown and there is a lack of outreach.

There are hundreds of such discouraged and struggling churches today in the mainline denominations. They present a special challenge to interim ministry, an opportunity to become revitalized through the interim process and developmental tasks. Congregations during the time between settled pastors are more open to change than at any other time. A committed partnership with a skilled interim pastor can greatly improve a congregation's attitude about itself and its approach to the future under a new pastor.

Lagging Stewardship Is Being Experienced

Howard was chairperson of the church finance board at Calvin Memorial Church. Concerned by the deficits being reported by the treasurer month after month, he requested a consultation with the newly arrived interim pastor.

"If it weren't for the income from our endowed funds, we would have to look for a part-time pastor," said Howard. "What is going on? Why aren't our people keeping up their pledges?"

It is not unusual for interim congregations to have a crisis of stewardship. In a day when many mainline congregations struggle with finances, it stands to reason that congregations between pastors may experience the problem more acutely. If there has been conflict, some contributors vote with their purse strings, and their giving declines "until things are more to our liking." Although no committed believer likes this idea of withholding financial support, it is a reality all the same. It is well accepted in fund-raising circles that "money follows interest and involvement in most human organizations." If conflict, boredom, or disillusionment have set in to a congregation's life, an erosion of financial support will be a symptom of such dynamics, along with a general decline in participation at worship or in fellowship activities.

There are other reasons for decline of stewardship as well. Keen observers of the religious scene today note a crisis of stewardship in mainline denominations. The stewardship philosophy of older generations is no longer being practiced by younger generations.

Many interim congregations need to make renewed stewardship a high priority, working with the interim pastor to marshall denominational resources for stewardship education and planned-giving programs. It is well accepted, of course, that stewardship involves more than the raising of money. It is concerned with the consecrated use of all resources for

God's work, including the time and talents of all members. A key objective of the interim process is the discernment of a new identity and mission. As members become involved in congregational self-assessment programs, and as new mission challenges begin to emerge, there will be renewed commitment of resources in support of a commonly held vision. As members come to feel more needed and interested, their giving increases.

Rebuilding the Infrastructure May Be Needed

Eleanor had been elected moderator of Zion Church only three months before the pastor announced his decision to leave after a pastorate of 14 years. During the interview with the prospective interim pastor, Eleanor was embarrassed not to be able to answer several questions that the interim candidate asked about the church organization and the roles of various leaders. She realized that there were actually no written position descriptions. She also became aware that there were no job descriptions for church employees. The departed pastor had always told everyone what to do. The congregation had been totally dependent on its leader.

Many interim congregations are emerging from such a leadership style. The lay leaders are in need of intensive training about their various functions and duties. The interim time is often a period when a congregation takes back control of its life and program from a Herr Pastor, a strong and dominant clergy leader. Some congregations discover that their by-laws need to be completely revised and brought up to date. I remember a congregation I served where the by-laws had not been changed in 50 years! A common characteristic of the interim congregation is a need to work on its infrastructure to improve the way things get done.

Leadership training may be the order of the day, helping lay leaders understand their various roles and improving their skills at such things as developing agendas, keeping good records, and running efficient meetings. One of my most satisfying experiences in work with more than 20 interim congregations has been the fun of seeing the laity take enthusiastic and effective control of their own church's organizational life.

Developing Communication Channels Is Vital

Russell was dismayed one Sunday to read in the weekly bulletin of Trinity Church that a congregational meeting would be held after the worship service.

He whispered to his wife, "Did we get a notice about this in the mail?"

"It's a surprise to me," she replied.

At the meeting Russell protested that due notice had not been given. Some members said that they had been aware of the meeting since the last council session. Other members said they only read about it in the morning's bulletin.

"The communication around this place leaves a lot to be desired," said Russell, with a tone mingling frustration and resignation.

Efficient and effective communication is a major concern of every congregation, and never more so when a vacancy occurs in the pastoral office. Interim congregations often discover that their communication system is very inadequate, resulting in poor decision-making processes and in misunderstandings. A strong congregation is one in which all information is freely shared and all members are fully informed and aware of church matters. Power struggles result when information is withheld as a means of controlling the organization. The interim time is a crucial opportunity for a congregation to examine its practices and ensure that an open system of communication and decision making is in place at the start of a new pastorate.

Ambivalence about Change Will Be Present

Rosalee and Phyllis were sharing a cup of coffee following their aerobics class at the parish house of United Church. The pastor had retired a few weeks earlier and the interim pastor had led her first service the day before.

"I liked her a lot," said Phyllis. "But I told her things were just fine here and I hoped she didn't plan on changing things."

Rosalee smiled and gave a little laugh as she said, "I liked her, too, but I told her that some things here need changing. So she got it from both sides. I think that's funny. Don't you?"

Interim congregations contain a mixture of feelings about change. For many, the departure of the former pastor is change enough, not to mention the temporary new face in the pulpit. Some will resist any effort to add or subtract programs, practices, or traditions. They want to preserve the status quo, either out of loyalty to the pastor who has gone or because they value things as they are. For some people all change is threatening. Phyllis sounds like such a person, and she represents many in the typical interim congregation. But there are also people who are ready for change, eager to try new things, and open to possibilities about a different future. They do not despise tradition, but neither do they want to be enslaved to it at the expense of innovation and discovery. Rosalee sounds like a representative of this segment of the interim congregation.

It may be helpful to keep in mind that the typical interim congregation has two agendas that run parallel to each other, not unlike a railroad track. One agenda is the regular agenda of every congregation and includes worship services, the sacraments, weddings, baptisms, confirmation, and funerals. The life and business of the congregation does not stop when the pastor leaves. The sick must be cared for and the shut-ins visited. Spiritual nurture of the young and the older members must continue. At the same time, the interim agenda must be furthered with careful attention to the developmental tasks of the in-between time. Change will probably be needed in some areas of congregational life. Such change will need to be carefully considered, and the widest possible acceptance of it sought in the membership. The important thing about change is that it should be the congregation's change, not something imposed by the interim leader. As little change as possible is a good rule, but when change is truly needed, it must be managed with sensitivity, openness, and good humor.

Mixed Emotions Will Be Present

After two meetings with the confirmation class of St. John's Church, the interim pastor decided he needed to have a personal talk with Matthew, a tenth-grader who had yet to say one word in the class and who seemed withdrawn and unhappy.

Drawing Matthew aside, he asked, "Don't you want to be part of confirmation, Matthew? I notice that you don't seem to participate in class discussions. Would you care to talk about it?"

The interim pastor got an immediate answer.

"I'm only here because my mom insists," said Matthew. "I liked Pastor Thomas a lot. He was cool. They gave him a raw deal asking him to leave."

There will be present in any interim congregation a host of feelings, most of them near the surface. If the previous pastor's departure was forced, some people will feel relief and others resentment. If the pastorate had been long and happy, there will be a pervasive sense of loss coupled with satisfaction at a job well done. There will be anxiety about the future and frustration about the present with its unaccustomed newness. There will be impatience and a desire to fill the opening as quickly as possible so as not to lose ground. There will be a sense of relief among those wanting a sabbatical from responsibility or a chance to be less involved, and there will be a sense of opportunity among those who have waited for a chance to be more active. There will be apprehension about the possible loss of members and of pledges. People will wonder who will do baptisms, weddings, and funerals.

Congregations are very complex organizations. A seasoned observer once described a congregation as being made up of three types of members. There are those who make things happen; those who let things happen; and those who wonder what happened. Although some might say such a comment verges on the cynical, my experience in 15 years of interim ministry in a variety of congregations tends to confirm this commentary about churches. An active corps of members will respond to a pastoral change with energy and passion. A second tier of members will be more passive, while still keenly interested in developments. A third segment of members will verge on indifference and assume that others will take care of the situation and that all will be well. Small wonder that a plethora of feelings whirl around in the typical interim congregation, especially at the beginning of the journey! Skilled interim ministry will enable a congregation to weather the somewhat bewildering mix of emotions and, in the course of the interim process, bring them, for the most part, to resolution. The interim congregation is indeed an exciting setting for ministry, and the interim period a time filled with potential and opportunity for creative growth.

For Reflection and Discussion

1. Do any of the characteristics described above seem evident in your congregation? Is there one that seems particularly pertinent?

2. If you were asked to describe your congregation as it enters the interim period, what characteristics would you cite?

3. What adjectives might you use to describe your congregation at this juncture in its journey? List as many as you can.

4. How would you finish the following sentence? "As I think about my church today, I feel . . ."

CHAPTER 3

The Church in Transition as a Human System

David R. Sawyer

Problem Person or Problem in the System?

A staff person fires off an angry letter to the personnel committee after being informed that her salary for the coming year will not be significantly increased. She is particularly unhappy because she has taken on added responsibilities in the past three months. The personnel committee chair is angry and concludes that this staff member is a "problem employee." The interim pastor, having decided that this staff member is making a valuable contribution to the life of the church, loses a couple of nights' sleep due to anxiety about the possibility of losing a significant colleague.

However, there is a larger picture to see. After calmer reflection, the interim pastor and the personnel committee come to recognize the "systemic problems" that underlie the current emotional eruption over a staff member and her salary.

The personnel committee has been preoccupied with redefining the personnel system and rewriting the personnel manual. Such activities are certainly helpful and appropriate during an interim time. Unfortunately, the members of the committee and the interim pastor overlooked the need to do a performance review and salary review with this particular staff member whose anniversary of employment came and went without recognition. When the interim pastor investigated the situation further, it became clear that the church did not have a salary administration plan in place. There were no policies or structures that described salary ranges and market comparisons for particular positions. With adequate salary administration policies in place, the personnel committee and the staff member, as well as the congregation, would know what the normal expectations for increases would be at a given time.

The systems perspective reduced the emotionality of the situation for the pastor and the committee. Fortunately, their calm response to the employee assisted her in recovering her balance as well. Solutions to a potential crisis began to flow more freely as anxiety decreased. That's a system in transition!

Without seeing things "whole," the occasion of an angry letter could have destabilized a congregation to the detriment of everyone. In some settings such emotional upset can end the ministries of other staff members and even the pastor. The pastor in this illustration was able to utilize an approach called systems thinking to help the committee and the staff see the ways in which people and actions are connected to each other, and thereby was able to help keep the congregation healthy during the time of transition.

The Sources for a Systems Approach

In my work as an interim pastor, I have had many occasions to give thanks for my awareness of systems thinking. When I was a graduate student in the early 1970s, I was introduced to "family systems therapy" as a method for helping families stay healthy. As I studied the method, I kept thinking to myself that there must be a way of building a bridge from family systems to helping churches stay healthy. The 1985 publication of Edwin Friedman's *Generation to Generation: Family Process in Church and Synagogue* supplied the bridge. People in church circles, and especially interim pastors, began shifting from linear-rational thinking to the circular thinking of the systems theory. Since that time, the courses in preparation for interim ministry provided by the Interim Ministry Network and by several denominations have encouraged pastors to see a congregation as a large, complex family. When Ed Friedman died in 1997, many interim pastors noted his passing with sorrow at the loss of such an important mentor, and felt gratitude for what he had taught.

In addition to the family therapists, other valuable sources for systems thinking can be found among management theorists such as Peter Senge and Margaret Wheatley, and even among quantum physicists such as Fritjof Capra. Systems thinking has become an important building block for much of current understanding of the world and human society.

Systems Thinking

Traditional scientific thinking made its contribution to the world by
taking things apart. Seeking ever smaller component parts and tracing
the lines of causation among them has been the approved method for
biology, psychology, and theology. In this century thinkers in nearly
every field have begun to see things whole. Instead of analyzing (which
means literally "to take apart"), they have been correlating, which suggests finding the patterns of relationships. In correlating we have learned
to recognize the indivisibility of systems. Solar systems and galaxies (at
the macro end of the spectrum) and subatomic particles (at the micro
end) all have connections with each other. Our understanding of any one
of these systems can be enhanced if we see them in their larger context.

Nearly everyone carries around an illustration of this new way of
understanding the world. In your purse or billfold, on at least one of your
credit cards, is a tiny, three-dimensional image called a hologram. The
hologram is to systems thinking what photography is to the classical,
scientific method. As you know, photography is created when light reflected directly from an object is recorded on film. The resulting image
is made up of tiny dots representing the parts of the original object. If
you look at one tiny spot on a photographic image with a microscope,
you will see only a small part of the original object. Although few
people really understand how it works, I have been taught to explain
holography as a process by which laser light is simultaneously bounced
off an object and beamed directly to a plate. In the resulting image, the
whole of the object is enfolded in each part of the image. View the
image in any small part and one can get a picture of the whole. By way
of analogy, a whole is not the sum of its parts; every part of a system is
the sum of the whole.

In systems thinking, a church, like every other system in the universe, can be understood as an indivisible whole that is bound together
by invisible, emotional connections. A church is a system of human (and
divine) relationships. Each congregation is its own bundle of relationships among people—its history, its vision, and its limitations. Like the
hologram, you can examine a congregation in any one of its constituent
parts and discover there a description of the whole congregation.

When leaders in the church understand the concept that everything
is related to everything else in a church, and that every part reflects the

whole, their perspectives change. They are no longer able to accept simple, single-cause explanations of church behavior. As a result, it is harder to find fault with any individual, or even with any single group, for any particular difficulty that a church is experiencing.

At the same time, seeing things whole goes against the usual and customary ways in which most people perceive the world (although people who were born after 1968 are more likely to take a holistic approach). It helps to recognize some of the universal characteristics of systems that can be found in a human system like a church. Systems thinking plays a particularly important role in understanding the ups and downs of a congregation during the interim time.

Organizational Structures

Probably the easiest way to begin to understand systems thinking is to look at structure. In systems thinking, the patterns in the makeup of the system are evidence that everything is connected with everything else. Structure reminds us that the organization is defined as a whole. Each fragment has the design of the whole enfolded within it.

> Structure may be *defined* as the arrangement, positioning, and relationships among the component parts of a system.

Structures may vary from church to church and from denomination to denomination, but there are universal patterns of structures. There are formal or overt structures, and there are also informal or covert structures. Since everything is interconnected, structures are always a good place to start in helping a human system become healthier. Three structural patterns—subsystems, triangles, and boundaries—are uncomplicated ways of seeing the connections between things in a church system.

Subsystems

The congregation is a larger system that serves as the context for its members and their families and for the groups and organizations within the congregation, both formal and informal. Each subsystem operates as a part of the whole and carries the design of the whole in its own unique makeup.

Subsystems may be *defined* as the component organizational units that are maintained by rules, by roles, and by rituals.

Examples of the rules by which a subsystem functions include attendance requirements, such as who can be a member and who cannot; how the leader of the group is chosen and treated; and to what extent information about what happens inside the group is shared with others outside the group. Every subsystem has particular roles which members of the subsystem play when interacting with each other. In addition to the leader, who may be the chairperson, the president, the director, or the convener, other roles might include the keeper of traditions, the challenger of traditions, the person who ensures that everybody is getting their needs met, and the person who keeps the collective nose to the grindstone by reminding everyone of the tasks that need to be accomplished.

A subsystem is also characterized and held together by its rituals. Some rituals are formal, such as the election and induction of a leader, or a particular way of doing prayers at the beginning or end of a meeting. Other rituals are informal. Such rituals include being sure there is always something chocolate to eat at every meeting, or an ongoing joke that is played on one member or another at each meeting. The rules, roles, and rituals are unique to each group, but they will always echo the way things are done in the church as a whole.

The choir is clearly a subsystem of the whole, even though it sometimes operates more independently. The Sunday school and each class within the Sunday school are subsystems of the whole. The church board and each of its committees, as well as the informal social gatherings and political affiliations among members, are also component parts of the larger whole. Whenever something happens with one of the subsystems that seems hard to understand, the systems thinker remembers to look for connections and parallels with other parts of the system.

In one church I know, for example, the interim pastor soon realized that the staff seemed to be always squabbling about something. The congregation was constantly worried about why their loving and competent staff members could not get along with each other. When the interim pastor helped the personnel committee to think systemically, they began to realize that the staff was actually acting out the conflicts between three groups in the church that held divergent views on the basic purpose of the church. Instead of those groups quarreling with each other or with the pastor, the conflict was projected onto the staff. Recognizing that the staff was indeed a subsystem of the whole did not immediately resolve the staff conflicts, but it did help remove the stigma that the staff members were "the bad ones." Every church is made up of two or more subsystems that interact—with each other and with the church as a whole—in ways that reflect the nature and character of the system.

Triangles

A second structural pattern that can be used to see connections in a church setting is triangles. Family therapists introduced the idea that triangles are the basic structure of human interaction.

> Triangles may be *defined* as three individuals or groups of individuals who interact in a pattern that may or may not be balanced.

Most relationships exist in threes instead of just twos. One reason for this is that a two-person relationship often generates anxiety between the two. Instead of resolving the anxiety directly, the tendency is to bring in another person or thing on whom to project the anxiety. Sometimes it's easier to talk about an important person in our lives to someone else instead of talking directly to the important person.

There is nothing inherently wrong with creating triangles. Triangles can be healthy or unhealthy. The healthy triangle is one in which the three members move easily around the triangle. That happens when the person in corner A sometimes talks to the person in corner B about the person in corner C, and sometimes person A talks to person C about person B. In the same way, a healthy triangle has shifting connections involving all three components. Triangles become unhealthy structures when two corners always side with each other against the remaining corner so that the third corner consistently becomes the "odd one out." A quick way to assess the health of a congregation during the interim period is to chart some of the triangles that are operating among the people or groups and determine whether or not the triangles within that system are balanced and flexible.

Boundaries

The third structural pattern has come more into public awareness in recent years. Often people talk about "boundary violations" in church relationships. These occur when the roles and rules of the system are not honored.

> Boundaries may be *defined* as the invisible, permeable, emotional borders marking the subsystems of a church. Boundaries limit access to relationships, information, and decision making.

Leaders of a congregation in a time of transition need to recognize and appreciate the boundaries of the major subsystems in order to enhance the health of the system. Here are some questions that might be asked to assess the health and effectiveness of the boundaries of the board:

- Is access to relationships, information, and decisions limited to those with formal involvement with the board?
- Are relationships among board members honored with honesty and integrity, without keeping secrets or sabotaging each other's work or personhood?
- Is confidential information that is discussed by the board repeated indiscriminately among other members of the congregation?
- When the board makes decisions appropriate to its authority and according to the rules and roles of the system, do church members abide by those decisions?
- Do any informal groups or individuals have the power to overrule the board's actions?
- To what extent do members know that their concerns will be received and heard by the board and that the board will consider them in light of the good of the whole church, even though the board may or may not do what a particular member wants it to do?

When boundaries are crossed on a regular basis, the whole system suffers. Working to improve boundary issues is often a significant part of the work of an interim pastor.

Stories

From a systems perspective, structures are the patterns of intercon-
nectedness in the organization. These patterns may be formal or informal, or overt or covert, but they *can* be identified, and health can be
encouraged through them. Another way of looking at a congregation as
a system involves listening to the stories the members tell about their
church. Physicists tell us that there is evidence of consciousness in the
smallest elements of the universe and in the largest. Since consciousness
appears to be present in most forms of life, the assumption is that both
consciousness and matter share roles as basic elements of the cosmos.[1]
Consciousness includes thought, feeling, desire, will, and memory.

Stories are the way a congregation gives voice to its consciousness.
Every congregation has prevailing myths, symbols, themes, and plots by
which it knows itself. The interim period is a good time to gather and
share stories of the congregation. Remember former pastors and how
they influenced the present life of the church. Recall times of elation
and times of difficulty and consider how the plot line of the church's
story shifted, thickened, or resolved itself in those times. During the interim time, church leaders need to pay close attention to periods of the
church's history that no one wants to talk about. That does not mean that
there is no story there. Rather, it means that the story of that period is so
highly significant in the life of the church that it needs to be told.

The degree of health in the system is usually indicated by the extent
to which the stories are aligned with the actual functioning of the system
—in other words, whether it works the way we tell ourselves it works. It
may be helpful to reframe the story to bring it more into alignment with
reality.

Three Systems Skills to Cultivate for the Interim Period

Structures and stories are two major characteristics of systems that help
church people get through the interim time in a more healthy and more
faithful way. Thinking systemically is a shift in seeing what is happening and a shift in responding to what is seen. Three skills of vision and
response have been an immense help to me in working with churches in
the interim period.

Skill 1. Seeing the process as well as the content. A major advantage of thinking systemically about churches is the mental framework for recognizing different levels of activity in the emotional system. The first skill for such sorting out is the ability to see process as well as content.

> Content is *defined* as the issue on which a conflict is focused—the "apparent" problem, the *what*.

> Process is *defined* as the structure of relationship beneath the conflict—the "underlying" problem, the *how*.

The cue to the presence of deeper process issues beneath the content of a conversation is emotional intensity. When reason and ease characterize the emotional intensity of an issue, one needs to attend primarily to the content issue—what it is we are talking about.

Let's imagine that the interim time opens a discussion about what time to schedule the summer worship services that generally change to an earlier hour during June, July, and August. In this case the content is the worship schedule. If the emotional tone is calm, factual, and moving toward easy resolution based on the needs of the congregation and the interests of the leaders, the focus of the conversation for everyone will primarily be the content issue.

If, however, the emotional intensity of the discussion changes to include anger, blame, or fear, then the systems thinking person will start looking for the process issues that have come into play. One looks for a history of interpersonal issues between members of the group; for needs for power, achievement, or affiliation; for loyalties to old schedules or attitudes; and for healthy and unhealthy triangles. Perhaps the head of the education committee took a major cut in the budget at the previous meeting and would feel hurt if the worship committee had all of its proposals approved. It may be that the choir feels slighted because the proposed schedule change puts more stress on the already overworked volunteer singers. Ordinarily, church folks pay some attention to these process issues without thinking about them, if things are going smoothly.

The wise systems thinker might assist the discussion by pointing out the presence of such unexpected emotion on so basic an issue. She or he might ask, in an open-ended way, what the group thought might be the underlying process issues that were preventing the group from handling the discussion as effectively as usual. At the very least, seeing the process as well as the content helps the systems thinker stay calm during a heated discussion.

Skill 2. Seeing parallels at different levels of the system. When a strange or unique pattern of behavior shows up in the church as an organization, systems thinking suggests that the same pattern is likely to be found at another level of the system as well. This skill refers back to the structural concepts of subsystems. Every system is a context for other subsystems and is itself a subsystem in a larger context.

When a congregation I consulted with several years ago began having open conflict of a particularly emotional and personal nature, I began wondering about what else was happening in the lives of the members of the church. Based purely on systems thinking (the whole is enfolded in each part), I started looking for parallels. Specifically, I suspected that some of the households in the congregation might be experiencing family problems during this time. With my eyes open to that possibility, I encouraged the interim pastor to listen for signs of family problems that might be revealed during pastoral care.

A couple of months later, the interim pastor reported that, indeed, among the most vocal participants in the conflict, one family was headed by an active alcoholic, another couple was teetering on the brink of divorce, a third household was in crisis over the drug addiction of one of their teenage children, and in a fourth family the breadwinner had just lost a job. Significant pain in one part of the system had overflowed into the larger system. At the same time, the congregational system had contributed to further stress in the families. I suggested that the emotional level of the conflict in the church could be possibly diminished if the interim pastor or one of the lay leaders provided some care and support to those troubled families. Looking for parallels can be a real source of help for anyone who wants to make churches healthier during the interim time.

Skill 3. Responding with playfulness instead of seriousness. A third skill that is particularly useful in times of stress and instability is the gift of a playful response. Churches are aided by members and leaders who adopt an attitude of "sitting light to oneself." Playfulness is not necessarily the same thing as use of humor, although good humor can be a part of a playful spirit.

Playfulness can be *defined* as chosen behavior characterized by surprise, humor, or reversal, and intended to continue a relationship without being controlled or controlling. Playfulness moves the system forward.

Seriousness can be *defined* as behavior drawn from predetermined roles, rules, and rituals, arising from anxiety and intended to get the upper hand in interactions by controlling or by avoiding being controlled. Seriousness holds the system back.

The skill of responding with playfulness was evident one day during a staff meeting to discuss the church youth program. The meeting was interrupted when the woman in charge received a call informing her that her daughter, who happened to be the president of the church youth group, had cut school that day. The mother reacted with anger. She immediately excused herself from the meeting while muttering about what she was going to do to punish her teenage daughter when she found her.

Her committee members at first responded with seriousness. They affirmed her concern on the one hand, but on the other hand they earnestly tried to persuade her to go easy on the young woman since she was known to be a good and mature member of the youth group. The more the colleagues matched the leader's seriousness with their own, the more angry and determined she became.

At the last moment, as she was walking out the door, one of her colleagues did a reversal and said, "Give her hell for me, too!"

The youth worker turned around, smiled, and said, "Yeah! Gotcha."

As the story illustrates, seriousness makes for more seriousness. By contrast, the playfulness of the last two responses helped the mother relax a little and get some perspective on her situation. The colleague's comment "turned into the skid" by lightly advocating something neither the speaker nor the youth worker really wanted. But it indicated a respect for her right to do whatever she chose, rather than what the group wanted her to do. Thus it was not controlling, but freeing in order to keep the relationship open. Seriousness works like a self-regulating cycle to keep the system operating in the same way. If the system is working in healthy ways, such stability can be good. If the system is not healthy, the self-regulating cycles only prevent healing. Playfulness breaks that restraint on the system and allows it to move forward toward more satisfactory levels of interaction that are better for all the members.

A Focus on Health

Systems thinking offers a helpful way of looking at churches. One of the results of this perspective has been that the church has been able to find a positive approach to understanding itself in times of transition. Most writers and leaders in the field of human-systems development hold a central value that organizations (families, churches, corporations) aspire to health and growth and well-being. Interim pastors and denominational leaders and consultants sometimes take the approach of focusing on what is going wrong with churches. Systems-thinking church people are able to focus on what is promoting growth in healthy and evolving churches.

Through the research and consultation that I have done in churches, as well as through my own leadership in churches and church organizations, I know that a knowledge of the universal characteristics of human systems can be used to help churches which are stuck in unhealthy patterns. It takes great courage and creativity to find the system leverage to move a church forward toward health and wholeness. But such effort, although not always fully successful, almost always helps the systems thinker become more healthy and whole.

For Reflection and Discussion

1. Identify two subsystems in your congregation. Name one or two of the rules, roles, and rituals that define and maintain each of those subsystems.

2. What characteristics of the whole system do you see enfolded in each of these subsystems?

3. Identify three triangles in your congregation. Are they healthy or unhealthy? Why?

4. How could the unhealthy triangles be made healthier?

5. Identify a situation in your congregation in which boundaries are clear and honored, and another situation in which they are vague or ignored.

6. How could your congregation become healthier about its boundaries?

7. Think of one or two stories about your congregation. How do these stories reflect the way your church functions?

8. Which of the three systems skills (seeing process and content, seeing parallels, responding with playfulness) do you personally most need to sharpen during the interim time in your congregation?

9. Name other leaders in your congregation who possess other systems skills. How can you encourage them to use their skills for the overall health of your congregation?

CHAPTER 4

Understanding Conflict and Power

Terry E. Foland

Conflict and power are normal elements of life in congregations. Problems occur when conflicts get out of reasonable control or when power is used to manipulate individuals or groups in the church to the advantage of one person or group and to the disadvantage of others.

The interim time provides an opportunity to focus on specific conflicts or misuse of power and to bring health to the congregation by enhancing the ability of the members and leaders to work together effectively. During an interim, however, there are also factors that may work against the ability of leaders to address issues of conflict and power.

In many cases, the pain of the conflicts may be at a sufficient level to warrant seeking some resolution; however, if the pain is too intense, leaders often cannot cope with trying anything new. They prefer to tolerate the pain rather than face the unknown. In other cases, leaders may be willing to accept the fact that there are critical problems or issues which need to be resolved, but they may feel that the real crisis is over because its "source"—the previous pastor—has gone. Some lay leaders may be willing to deal with conflict without the help of a called pastor and therefore are able to resolve problems during the interim; others may be tempted to wait for the next pastor to be their "savior." In some congregations leaders recognize that during an interim the "time is ripe" to deal with critical issues of conflict and power struggles, while other leaders may view the interim as a respite from the fray of the battle.

Church leaders might not feel ready to address problems of conflict and power, but it is important that the issues be addressed during the interim period and not be left to be resolved after a new pastor arrives.

To begin a new ministry relationship with unresolved conflict in the church will probably not bode well for the future!

Definitions

Conflict may be defined in a number of ways. I will be talking about it as contradictory points of view, or struggle for limited resources. Conflict is a major disagreement that causes tension in the life of the community of the church. Conflict sometimes involves people who tend to be argumentative, but it may also involve an appropriate clash of beliefs, goals, interests, or needs of people in the church.

Power may be defined as "the ability to act or do." Power is the ability either to make things happen or to keep them from happening—to get others to comply with one's wishes or to block the actions of others.

Both conflict and power are neutral terms. The plus side of conflict is that its presence may indicate that something important is happening in the church, or that something important needs to happen, or that the accomplishment of something important is being threatened. There is usually high interest in a matter that has more than one possible outcome. Managed carefully, conflict helps bring about needed change in the congregation.

The downside of conflict is that it can be divisive and cause people to feel hurt and discounted. Conflict may divert energy and resources away from productive ministry and mission. People in conflict tend to have skewed perspectives on the issues. They often react in ways they normally would not, or they believe things about others they would not normally believe. People in conflict skew data they receive; they misinterpret the beliefs, actions, and words of those with whom they are in conflict; and they break off communication with the opposition, except to attack or attempt to convince them that they are wrong.

The positive aspect of power is that it makes things happen. Issues of power in the church are usually about control or fear. Control is about how things get done or get stopped. Fear is usually an indication that one is concerned about pending change or about losing something of value. Positive use of power helps the community of the church to function well and effectively. Negative use of power causes the community of the church to malfunction or misuse its resources. Negative power is usually narrow in focus and manipulative in action. Positive use of power calls forth openness and invites participation of the members of the faith community in decision-making processes. Negative use of power seeks to limit the involvement of those who may be included in decision-making processes.

What Are Church Fights About?

Although church conflict or power issues may be about almost anything, there are a few basic areas today which are major sources of strife in congregations.

Church Identity

Fights about identity may reflect a fear of losing place or status as a church in the community. They may express the anxiety members have about the future. The identity issue is about who we are now and what we understand our purpose and mission to be in this time and place. What do we understand as the purpose and mission of the congregation? How will we relate to the denomination? How should we divide mission dollars between local outreach and national or world outreach?

At Trinity Church the congregation was still living out its identity from the decade of the 1960s. They had been in the first wave of congregations to be intentional about being integrated, having welcomed African Americans to join their all-white church. They were intentional about calling a woman pastor (they claim the first woman pastor of their denomination), thus giving emphasis to the rights of women as leaders in the church. More recently, they have been among the leaders in their denomination to affirm gays and lesbians as people who can participate fully, with no reservations, in the life of their congregation.

But Trinity Church found that this identity of being "out front on social issues" was no longer attracting people to join. In their case, one of their strongest assets as a church was also a liability. The leadership struggled with how to move to a new identity that would still value what they had believed, but that would not be a turnoff to potential new members. They agreed upon three shifts to help with that change in identity: (1) a shift from a church seeking to be integrated, to a church seeking to be in partnership with black congregations; (2) a shift from an image of having a leadership comprised only of women, to an affirmation that men and women can be equal as leaders; and (3) a shift from a reputation of being a gay church, to being a church tolerant of many views on sexuality.

Who Is in Charge?

This issue may manifest itself in a struggle between the clergy and the lay leadership, or between formal or informal leaders in the church. Many members of churches today believe they have the "right" to know what is going on in church governance and that they also have the "right" to have some voice in decisions affecting them as members. The positive element of that attitude is healthy involvement. The negative element is unhealthy interference with appropriate, orderly processes that may require some degree of privileged information.

This occurred at New Hope Church, where the pastoral relations committee had to deal with a sensitive issue regarding the appropriateness of touching and hugging by the pastor. Some members got wind of the issue and called a meeting of friends to force the issue out into the open. When the issue became public, some of the pastor's antagonists convinced several women that they were being sexually abused. The women were pushed to file sexual misconduct charges with the denominational office against the pastor. Before there was a proper investigation, word spread among the congregation that the pastor was having sexual relations with some church members. The pastor resigned out of anger. The investigation by the sexual misconduct committee of the denomination resulted in the conclusion that the pastor was not guilty of misconduct, but that he would benefit from counseling regarding his need to touch and hug. There was probably no reason for the pastor to leave New Hope since he had the support of at least 90 percent of the congregation. However, under the guise of "rights," a few people had the power to cause him to leave. If the situation had been handled by the pastoral relations committee and the board, the results would probably have been much different.

What Do We Believe?

This fight may be about how a church interprets the Bible or about what curriculum is taught to the children and youth. It may have to do with lifestyles or social issues and the church's stand on those issues. The issue may be about how people are helped with their own spiritual growth. What one group or an individual wants or needs may result in a clash with what other groups or individuals believe or feel they need or want.

St. Anne's Church resolved an issue of this sort by establishing two different tracks for Bible study. They began with the assumption that belief about the Bible could be on a continuum, with one end being biblical literalism and the other end being biblical interpretation. One Bible study group believes in the Bible as "direct word of God." Their members believe in the inerrancy of the Scriptures. The other group believes in the Bible as the unfolding story of the development of faith in the Jewish-Christian tradition. The two groups study the same texts and come together once a month to have open dialogue on what the texts mean for their lives today in the culture of their Midwestern city.

How Do We Worship?

Tensions often escalate around the distinction between traditional and contemporary worship. The type and style of music, preaching, dress, time of services, and how formal or informal the atmosphere is for worship are all part of this conflict. Attempts to compromise by including some aspects of the traditional or "old" forms of worship and some aspects of "new" forms may exacerbate the problem by offending everyone who prefers one style or the other.

At Church-on-the-Hill there was tension regarding the effort to blend traditional worship and contemporary worship. This conflict was resolved by holding two totally different services. One is strictly traditional; the other is entirely contemporary. They also decided that on fifth Sundays they would have only one service for everyone, alternating between traditional worship and contemporary worship. Also, on those fifth Sundays, they scheduled a fellowship time that provides an opportunity for people to discuss the worship experience. This pattern has now been in effect for two years and is working well for them.

Role Expectation of Leaders

Most often this issue focuses on the clergy or the program staff, but sometimes the focus is on the lay leaders and their roles and functions. The issue regarding clergy is often the result of confusion about the differences between leadership and management. The conflict may also have to do with the minister's and staff's use of time and priorities, and with who determines those time allocations and priorities.

The conflict may also be the result of either gaps or clashes. Gaps result when one person or group thinks that a task is someone else's responsibility and no one takes care of it. A clash results when more than one group or individual believes that they are responsible for a matter. A turf battle may then ensue. For example, calling on the shut-in members may be thought by the laity to be the responsibility of the pastor, while the pastor may feel it is the responsibility of the deacons. In order for that ministry to be effective, there needs to be an understanding of the partnership between clergy and laity. Without such an understanding, there will continue to be a gap, and one side will probably blame the other for the lack of ministry to the shut-ins.

Limited Resources

Conflict may be about the use of resources such as dollars, space, scheduling, or volunteers. When this kind of conflict arises, the congregation must return to its mission and goals for guidelines about allocating resources.

Focus Inward or Focus Outward?

Do we emphasize nurture and care of the membership, or service and care for those beyond the membership? Some people view the church as a provider of services or products and ask, "What can we get from this church?" Others view the church as a community that offers services and help to others. They ask, "What can we provide for those who are in need?" A fight might result from any effort to change the congregation's emphasis.

For example, should a church spend most of its resources on programs for nurturing the children and youth in the faith, or should they spend the limited resources on programs of social mission, such as feeding the hungry and helping to build better homes for the poor of the community? Many churches have found that they can do both, by providing programs for youth and adults who learn more about the faith as they work together on projects to help the poor.

Malfeasance or Misconduct by Clergy

Usually, when a pastor is accused of illegal, immoral, or unethical behavior, some people will readily believe the accusations and others will passionately defend the pastor. When such issues have been part of the ongoing life of a congregation, the agenda of the interim period must include dealing with a wide range of human feelings—anger, disgust, disappointment, guilt, remorse, trust, and forgiveness. Members will not all feel the same way at any given time. Indeed, an individual might feel several things at once, and various members' feelings might conflict with one another.

Signs of Unhealthy Conflict

Although conflict may be seen as a normal part of the life of a congregation, there are times when the conflict is simply not healthy and over time will cause harm to the church as well as to the parties caught up in the conflict. Following are some signs that usually indicate that conflict is being handled in an unhealthy manner:

- The anger being expressed seems more intense than the surface issue warrants. Undue anger is usually a warning sign that people are feeling mistreated, misled, or abused in some way. In healthy handling of conflict, people may exhibit anger and other strong emotions, but the level of anger and feelings expressed is congruent with the issue.
- The disputants cannot separate the issues from the people with whom they disagree. *People*, rather than issues, are the focus.

Healthy conflict will focus on what we want done or not done and how we are affected, rather than on who did or did not do something.

- The actions or beliefs of the opposition are viewed as sinful or morally wrong instead of as alternate ways of acting, a different viewpoint, or an alternate moral choice. Healthy conflict will allow for differences without judging those with whom we disagree.

- Communication is diminished, convoluted, or essentially nonexistent. The time when people need to increase the communication is often the time when they quit talking to each other. People in conflict tend to talk only *with* those with whom they agree and *about* those with whom they disagree. They also tend to interpret the communication of the opposition without checking meanings with the opposition. In healthy conflict there is adequate exchange of messages between the parties.

- Indications of vindictiveness will be prevalent in unhealthy conflict. People do and say things that are calculated to hurt others. Important past relationships are forgotten, and the focus is on winning at all costs, even if it means that some people will be hurt in the process. In healthy conflict, attempts are made to understand and empathize with the opposition.

- Disputants express a long list of issues or complaints and begin to recall other unresolved issues from the past. In healthy conflict the disagreement will stay focused on the main issue of the moment.

- People deny their real feelings about the conflict or about unresolved issues. A healthy attitude will allow people to be open about their feelings and about how they are affected by the continuing problem.

- People refuse to accept any solutions to the conflict. An objection is raised to any possible answer to the conflict. Parties do not want the conflict to be resolved but rather enjoy the fight and will do all they can to keep it going, regardless of the toll it may take on the congregation or on the individuals involved. In healthy conflict, disputants are committed to finding common ground and reaching a solution that satisfies the core needs and values of all concerned.

Using Conflict Constructively

Using conflict constructively means taking the energy and interest that people have invested in the conflict and letting them create something productive or useful. Following are some guidelines for using a conflict situation constructively:

- Embrace the conflict as an experience with the potential for something positive instead of viewing it as something fearful. Welcome conflict as a sign that there is something worth expending energy, time, and resources to resolve. View conflict as the agenda of the church for a brief period of time. Allow the conflict to be an experience through which people can grow and be transformed, rather than thwarted and diminished.
- Offer those being affected by the conflict opportunity for defining the issues and searching for the solutions. Take control of the situation by defining its purpose and developing a plan of action.
- Limit discussion to the real issues and do not allow other unrelated issues to be brought into the process. Acknowledge, however, that after the disputants have found a satisfactory solution to the defined issue, they may then be ready to work on other issues that have been identified in the course of the attempts to resolve the initial conflict.
- Assume that all parties who are engaged in the conflict bring some truth to the discussion. Assume also that everyone carries some misperceptions about what has happened or what is needed. Conflict is often the result of seeing and experiencing things differently. Value the differences.
- Seek to find the commonalities and build on them while valuing the differences.
- Emphasize finding answers that meet the needs and interests of all parties rather than focusing on specific positions.
- Make use of spiritual resources and frame the discussion as a discernment process, then allow time for the process to work. Do not try to meet some artificial deadline. Discernment takes time, patience, and openness.
- Work for agreements that are tolerable, even if not fully acceptable, to all people involved. The goal is a solution that all parties can support, even if they do not fully agree with it.

Living with Conflicts

Not all conflicts can be resolved. Sometimes the only answer is to nego-
tiate ways in which those in conflict can continue to live together. Such
a negotiation process should include not only the disputing parties, but
also representatives who can speak for those who are not directly involved but who are affected by the dispute. These people, who might be
called neutrals, have at least three functions to offer in such a process.

First, they offer the voice of the church-at-large regarding the dispute, helping the involved parties understand how "their" fight is affecting the entire life of the congregation.

Second, they offer a moderating influence in the negotiation process. Neutral parties can usually find areas of agreement that the disputants can "live with," thus avoiding a stalemate.

Third, the neutral members in the process help monitor the agreements and hold the disputants accountable for them.

Mediation might produce agreements such as: We agree not to be
disruptive of each other. We agree not to attack each other verbally or
physically in any gathering of the church. We agree not to spread false
tales or gossip about each other. We agree to check out the things we
hear about each other with the other party.

Other agreements might include both sides taking a sabbatical from
the dispute for a period of three months and then reconvening for further
dialogue on the issues that divide them.

Moving to Genuine Dialogue

When there is conflict in a church, those involved must engage in
dialogue rather than debate or discussion. Debate has particular ground
rules that encourage an adversarial stance. One wins a debate by presenting more positive points than the opponent and by attacking the
weak opponent's points. In a debate there will be a winner and a loser.
The legal court system in this country is based on such an adversarial
approach. In church conflict the goal should not be an end in which
there are declared winners and losers.

Discussion implies argument or "the hearing of ideas back and forth
until there is a winner." The Latin root of our word *discussion* has the

same root as the words *percussion* and *concussion*. It literally means using force to make a point. A percussion instrument is played by striking. A concussion is caused by a sharp blow to the head. We often hear people say something like, "We ought to knock some sense into them." Some people also seem to think that if they say something often enough, or loudly enough, the opposition will be persuaded. But this usually only causes the opposition to become louder and more persistent also. Forcefulness is normally met with equal or stronger forcefulness.

In his book *The Fifth Discipline* Peter M. Senge contrasts dialogue and discussion. Senge recalls that the Greek roots for the word *dialogue* are *dia*, meaning "through," and *logos*, meaning "word" or, more broadly, "meaning." The main idea of the word *dialogue* is a free flow of ideas between people.[1] This Greek word *logos* is the same word that the writer of the Gospel of John uses in his prologue. The "word," or *logos*, is the creative force that was with God at the time of creation and is the same word that became incarnate in Jesus Christ (John 1:1-14).

"Dia logos" is what we want to create in the church in times of conflict. "Dia logos" means that we enter into conversation with each other not only to state our perspectives, needs, and views, but also to genuinely hear the perspectives, needs, and views of others. More importantly, we open ourselves to the power of the "word" or spirit of God to enhance and enrich our conversation.

Peter Senge also observes:

> The purpose of a dialogue is to go beyond any one individual's understanding. . . . In dialogue, individuals gain insights that simply could not be achieved individually. . . . In dialogue, a group explores complex difficult issues from many points of view. Individuals suspend their assumptions but they communicate their assumptions freely. The result is a free exploration that brings to the surface the full depth of people's experience and thought, and yet can move beyond their individual views.[2]

Genuine dialogue is intended to help church leaders and members to make wise and "spirit-led" decisions.

Use of Spiritual Resources

In an unpublished study conducted by several consultants of the Alban
Institute in 1993 and 1994, it became apparent that most people who
are engaged in church conflict do not think of using spiritual resources
to help them resolve the conflicts. When people were asked to identify
the spiritual resources they drew on during the course of the church conflict, only a small percentage (about three to five percent) were able to
name any specific resources. Those who did recall spiritual resources
mentioned such things as praying together, Bible study, and meditation.
My experience with church people in conflict is that prayer and Bible
references are more often used as weapons than they are as strategies to
improve understanding or find resolution to the disputes. I have often
heard people pray that others might "see the light" and "reject their
sinful ways." Of course, "the light" happened to be the position taken
by the pray-er, and the "sinful ways" would be corrected if the "sinner"
were just like the praying "saint."
     Spiritual resources can be used intentionally to help those in dispute
to discern what the will of God might be in a given situation. Establishing times and processes to engage in genuine dialogue is such a spiritual
resource. Prayer that enables participants to examine themselves and
that calls for openness to understanding of each other is another spiritual resource. Careful study of a variety of scripture texts from a variety
of perspectives that open the subject to several different views is a spiritual resource. Guided meditation during the course of efforts to resolve
conflicts is another spiritual resource. During these moments people are
given the opportunity to "listen for the word or spirit of God." Seeking
the advice and counsel of scholars and various experts on the specific
conflict issues—again getting different perspectives—is another way
of using spiritual resources. Reading books on the conflict issues that
may give new insights to the disputants is another strategy for spiritual
guidance. People favoring different sides of the issue might suggest
materials for all to read. In addition to reading materials that reinforce
their own point of view, everyone should agree to read materials that
support the opposite point of view, with the expressed intent of increasing understanding and appreciation of the opposing side. An intentional
effort on the part of all people in conflict to use spiritual resources and
to work together to identify what those resources are and how they will
use them will be in itself a movement toward resolution of the conflict.

For Reflection and Discussion

1. Why is an interim period a good time to try to resolve conflict?

2. In what ways have you experienced conflict as a positive presence in your church?

3. The chapter identifies several issues about which there may be church conflicts. What would you add to the list?

4. What signs of unhealthy conflict have you observed in your church?

5. How have the spiritual resources of your church been used in times of conflict?

6. How can the concept of divergent answers to problems be useful to your church?

CHAPTER 5

The Interim Minister:
A Special Calling

Paul N. Svingen

Pastor Dave and his wife Mary were chatting over a final cup of coffee
before he left for the office.

"I've been thinking," he said. "In just three years I'll be 62. I could
retire then and ask Bishop Baldwin to find me an interim close to home.
That way we would have extra income to supplement my pension and
Social Security."

Who could argue that Pastor Dave shouldn't be entitled to the
small benefit of supplementary income following retirement? And who
would be surprised to hear that the recently retired neighborhood pastor
was now helping out, filling in, or just doing interim ministry at the
church down the road?

In a neighboring community three years later, the long-term pastor
at Valley Church left suddenly. As congregational leaders hurriedly
assembled a call committee, someone mentioned that the pastor of the
church in nearby Springfield had just retired. Who better than the "tried-
and-true" Pastor Dave to fill in for the few weeks or months it might
take to get a new permanent pastor? Plus, Valley Church could finally
reduce its long-standing budget shortfall, get ahead, and be in a more
solid financial position when the next permanent pastor arrived. This
could be an impressive new beginning for a congregation that had long
struggled to meet its obligations. Valley Church and Pastor Dave would
be helping each other. The congregation could save money; Pastor Dave
could supplement his retirement income.

Although this is the way interim ministry has been understood in
the past, things are much different today. Even though it is still true that
at the time of a pastoral vacancy most denominations allow congregations to call on any credentialed pastor in good standing to provide

them pastoral services on an interim basis, it is also true that congregations are increasingly intentional about how they choose to use the interim period. Sensitive lay leaders today are more keenly aware of the normal increase in anxiety that manifests itself in their congregation when they lose their pastor. No matter what the reason may have been for the pastor's termination, they see their fellow members exhibiting a mixture of strong reactions. More enlightened lay leaders are choosing to invest both in their church's future and in that of their next installed pastor, by seeking the pastoral and consultative services of trained and qualified interim ministry specialists.

One of the results of the new awareness by lay leaders of congregations in pastoral transition is the realization that many retired pastors, like Pastor Dave, are not as well-equipped to handle the congregation's unique need for interim, developmental leadership as was once thought to be the case. Lay leaders are also recognizing that there are many good pastors, both those who are approaching or already at retirement as well as younger pastors, who feel called to this specialized ministry and who could undertake interim ministry training. Depending on their gifts and skills, particularly their understanding of and insight about the emotional dynamics of the interim period, these trained pastors could become valuable and effective agents of change in congregations.

Intentional interim ministry is a challenging vocation that requires experienced pastors with particular gifts and abilities. The pastor who chooses interim ministry as a career has a particular set of leadership assets, skills that have been honed in the emotional field of congregations which have experienced the grief of change and loss. These leadership skills and abilities enable some pastors to be uniquely effective leaders in times of pastoral transition. These leadership gifts, combined with basic pastoral experience, have led to the recognition of this ministry as a particular calling—a specialized ministry just as vital as the specialized ministry of a chaplain, a missionary, a seminary professor, or a church consultant. Intentional interim pastors bring to congregations skills in the management of change, the ability to help members envision the future, and solid experience in pastoral ministry.

A Season and a Time

There is much agreement that the context for interim pastoral leadership is not unlike that of a wilderness. Intentional interim ministry requires a pastoral leader who is undaunted by situations in which surface structures have been stripped away and fundamental issues of faith and discipleship are more readily discernible. The late Edwin Friedman, a nationally recognized family therapist and rabbi, has observed that interim times are times in which the emotional system unlocks. Ministry takes on an intensity that is not usually experienced when a congregation is "settled in" with its long-term, installed, permanent pastoral leader. Intentional interim ministers see themselves as consultative leaders, and they accompany their congregations through a rich and varied territory by using both established and potential pathways to help these congregations pursue their vision of a mission under God.

Loren B. Mead, founder of the Alban Institute, realized that many congregations undergo an interim after a pastor leaves. He discovered a pattern regarding the length of pastoral calls: long-term calls were often followed by short-term calls. Mead wrote about the characteristics of this interim in a book entitled *New Hope for Congregations*.[1] These are components that congregational leaders need to know about and support so that the interim pastor's work can be properly interpreted to congregants who might otherwise overreact to an interim pastor who is doing more than would normally be expected of a "fill-in" pastor.

The six characteristics of intentional interim ministry are: (1) intentionally facing conflict, (2) using a problem-identification process, (3) using a "contract" to name the specific interim issues to be addressed mutually by interim pastor and congregation, (4) recognizing the presence and value of the unique personality and leadership style of the interim pastor, (5) viewing the interim pastor, in part, as a consultant, and (6) recognizing the need for planned termination and closure with the congregation. It has been my experience that in each of the 20 interim pastorates I have served, these six characteristics of intentional interim ministry have consistently emerged as components of the overall interim agenda.

Certainly any credentialed pastor in good standing can serve a given congregation between installed pastors. What distinguishes the ministry of the trained and experienced interim pastor is that she or he is

called into a congregation that has lost its installed pastor and has subsequently chosen to be intentional about how it utilizes the weeks,
months, or years of its forthcoming interim period. The congregational
leaders have chosen to be wise stewards of this often unplanned time
"between the no longer and the not yet."[2] The interim pastor recognizes
the uniqueness of this call and of her or his experience and interest.
Having had special training in this itinerant pastoral ministry, the interim pastor is equally intentional about serving a congregation that has
claimed its interim period as a God-given opportunity for reflection,
study, learning, renewal, and preparation for the future. That is, both the
pastor and the congregation are intentional about addressing the needs
and making good use of the gifts to be found in the interim time.

Ideally, intentional interim ministry requires a seasoned pastor who
has had a diversity of pastoral experience in more than one congregational setting. She or he has achieved a well-developed sense of pastoral
identity without having sacrificed either personal identity or those unique
leadership gifts needed for the kind of pastoral ministry that the interim
task requires. Deeply etched in my mind are five specific personal characteristics most assuredly identified with all pastors known for their
effectiveness in the congregational setting. In a sermon preached some
years ago, Dr. Morris Wee, then senior pastor of Central Lutheran Church
in downtown Minneapolis, boldly proclaimed that in order to be faithful
to the high calling of ordained ministry, all pastors need to be willing
and able to (1) love the Lord God; (2) love all people; (3) maintain
good health; (4) read a book; and (5) have and maintain a healthy sense
of humor. I have often thought that these five general characteristics of
pastors function as bedrock for the six specific characteristics previously
mentioned which frame the leadership agenda of the interim ministry.

A Matter of Stewardship

Given the characteristics of an effective interim ministry and the general
requirements of faithful ministry, what should congregations be able to
expect from an effective interim minister? Intentional interim leadership
requires adaptability and flexibility, particularly related to (1) the presence of various theological emphases; (2) leadership issues related to
"the what," "the how," and "the who" of ministry in individual congregations; (3) denominational relationships; (4) lifestyle and family issues

for the interim minister; (5) mobility issues that influence availability; (6) support issues that affect ongoing vocational viability; (7) career goals and continuing education; and (8) hands-on leadership issues relevant to the special needs of a given congregation.

In many cases, a congregation in transition requires the proven skills of a trained, interim pastor because it is fraught with intense and conflicting human emotions. Effectively working with the pulsating emotional processes of a congregation that has been wounded by grief, conflict, betrayal, or other emotions connected with transition requires a self-differentiated pastor who has a clear vision both of what the interim period and the interim minister are and are not about. Friedman has suggested that the pastor functioning as interim leader most needs to demonstrate a healthy balance as an emotional, social, psychological, rational, and spiritual being. She or he must function as a wise steward of self in the midst of a whirling mix of human behaviors. The pastor's responsible self-management reveals to the congregation genuine servanthood, faith-centeredness, and a spiritual stability that congregants recognize and trust as helpful during the interim. An intentional interim pastor will bring calmness, thoughtfulness, objectivity, trustworthiness, care, and mature leadership into this context of change. At the same time, the interim pastor will be flexible in his or her leadership style and in conflict management in a given congregation. Situations vary from church to church. What proved to be an effective leadership response in one interim setting may not necessarily be helpful in another setting.

Full Time Plus

Among the numerous misconceptions of what interim ministry is, a persistent one is that it is a retirement ministry. Intentional interim ministry is not a retirement ministry for pastors in the usual sense of retirement—work with fewer hours, less responsibility, less focus, and less intentionality. It is quite the opposite. The interim-leadership needs of a vital, mission-focused congregation that has lost its pastor, no matter what the circumstances, are not for less leadership, but for at least as much, if not more, leadership. Major attention must be given to issues that have surfaced in relation to the loss of a significant leader in a dynamic, living, grieving congregation. A human system is in trauma. All the emotions that an individual experiences in grief are present in a congregation that has suffered a significant loss. Adding the management of such acute dynamics to the ongoing, everyday work of the pastor requires much more than one ordinarily provides in a retirement ministry. Guiding a congregation through the interim is hard work. Congregations have a right, and perhaps an obligation, to expect an interim pastor who is willing and able to do this hard work.

Although many in our society thoughtlessly associate "permanent" with "full-time," and "temporary" or "interim" with "part-time," many, if not most, congregations experiencing pastoral change do need full-time ministry of Word and Sacrament. The health of the whole body requires additional resources and sometimes special, skilled attention to specific parts of the body. The balance and well-being of the whole body is achieved and maintained through wise and thoughtful responses to changes that have occurred as a result of the loss. For a congregation to respond to a loss of a pastor with a strategy to "get by" with less and hurry through the interim toward premature decisions about new leadership is unhealthy. Such a process of planting bad seeds will only lead to further loss and pain in the not-too-distant future. The long-held notion that the interim pastor is a retired pastor who "marks time" or simply "fills in" is being recognized by more and more lay people as inadequate to the basic developmental needs of congregations in search of new pastoral leadership.

Today an increasing number of effective parish pastors are taking stock of their gifts for ministry and considering how to best serve the church in the last phase of their careers. Many are looking at interim ministry, convinced that intentional interim ministry is a growing need in the church, as well as an opportunity for experienced pastors to be good stewards of their gifts. These men and women see their wide pastoral experience, their spiritual centeredness, and their ability to "manage self" as gifts that can be used to help congregations responsibly address pastoral transition. They understand that the whole church will benefit when they respond to the call to this ministry. Furthermore, the well-being of yet another clergy person and her or his family will have been enhanced. The whole of the church will be healthier and more able to embrace the call of the Gospel of Jesus Christ.

Continuity of Ministry and Support

Congregational leaders need to be aware of the many variables affecting
the choice and tenure of interim pastors. It is important to understand the
vocational realities with which interim pastors work. A pastor specializ-
ing in intentional interim ministry must be able to live and to serve in a
context of uncertainty. Although the contract, covenant, or letter of
agreement she or he has with the congregation and the denominational
office does indicate a target termination date, even the timing of that
date is dependent upon a number of factors outside the control of either
the interim pastor or the congregation. For example, a candidate-elect
may decide not to accept the congregation's call; thus, the interim period is extended. The developmental work of the interim period may be
abbreviated for some reason. For instance, the initial candidate's timely
acceptance and early availability would cause the interim period to be
shorter than planned. Sometimes circumstances are such that not all of
the developmental work of the interim period gets completed. More
often than not, however, and particularly if other pastors on a multi-
pastor staff are identified as viable candidates for the open position, the
interim period may well be longer than first thought. In any case, the
interim pastor must be a person willing and able to minister confidently
in a context of uncertainty.

Friedman suggests that throughout the duration of the interim period
there is a need for the interim minister to function as a "non-anxious"
presence. Sometimes, with assistance from the denomination, it is possible to predetermine the place and timing of the next interim pastorate
prior to the interim's departure from a congregation. When this is the
case, the interim pastor is more free to focus directly on pertinent termination issues and on the closure needs unique to the congregation in
which important ministry has occurred. Unfortunately, this ideal is not
always achievable, so lay leaders should be aware that the interim minister might be carrying such concerns.

Mobility and Self-Care

It is also important that congregational leaders, and members in general,
have some awareness of the unique lifestyle issues that relate to intentional interim pastors who move from church to church. Many interim

pastors accept calls to pastorates away from home. Across denominations today there is no shortage of congregations needing qualified,
intentional interim pastors. Still, although many established, career
interim pastors have long since recognized the necessity of having a
"home base," it is rare for an interim's home to be within the geographical boundaries of the interim parish. Therefore, while serving away from
home, the pastor must make provision for maintenance of family and
property needs. Intentional interim pastors typically put on a lot of high-
way miles and experience greater overall living and transportation costs
than do longer-term conventional pastors, sometimes even functioning as
their own travel agents in order to manage a significant commute by air.
In those situations in which the interim assignment prohibits a daily
commute from home, short-term housing arrangements must be made,
usually in a parsonage, apartment, or hotel.

Other dimensions of routine daily living such as eating, wardrobe
maintenance, daily exercising, conducting social life, and finding time
for rest and recreation are all part of what must be managed by the
itinerant interim pastor and his or her family. Oftentimes the abnormal-
ity and inconvenience of the interim pastor's need to perform normal
life functions away from home goes largely unnoticed by congregants
and is understandably taken for granted. Clearly, the interim pastor's
need to effectively manage self is truly multi-dimensional. When all is
said and done, an intentional interim pastor's work in the congregation
is not unlike that of a management consultant. Not only have the surface
structures in the congregation been stripped away, but many other familiar support structures for daily living have been interrupted or changed
in order that this interim ministry be accomplished for the sake of the
Gospel. Sensitivity by congregations to these aspects of interim ministry
will surely help the interim leader perform better and enhance the congregation's progress through the interim time.

The Gift of Networking

Within the context of the congregation's mission and ministry and the
related responsibilities and privileges shared by all ordained pastors, the
interim pastor must be more of a "networker" than is any pastor committed to the call of the Gospel and to the business of "fishing" for the souls

of women and men. As an intentional interim pastor to 20 congregations, as an interim consultant to several more, as an active member of and leader in the Interim Ministry Network for 15 years, and as a trainer of hundreds of interim pastor candidates from more than 20 denominations across the United States and Canada, it has been my joyful discovery to find a unique fellowship in the company of other clergy who have caught the vision of interim ministry. This fellowship is known as the Interim Ministry Network, a collegium of intentional interim pastors. The existence of the network is significant for lay leaders because it speaks to the commitment that the member pastors have for an unusual, but highly valuable, ministry.

As a result of my lengthy involvement in training, continuing education, annual conferences, leadership opportunities, and local support groups, I have realized that I am privileged to have been given the call to serve Christ as an interim pastor. It has been my experience that during the interim period, congregations are more open to change than at any other time. It is exciting to journey in faith with a congregation whose circumstances have provided it the opportunity to come to terms with its history, rediscover its identity, enable needed leadership changes, and rethink its vital connection to the larger church. I have discovered that in congregations facing change there is a vitality, a hopefulness, a readiness, and an expectant gratitude in recognition of God's intervention and grace. I have discovered again and again that congregations in transition are emergent with new lay leaders, new directions, new vision, and a renewed commitment to God's future with them.

Through my interdenominational association with many other interim ministers over the years, I have also realized that my "interim discoveries" were not exclusive to me. It has been fun to recognize and claim the fruits of genuine collegiality that serve as support and affirmation for this ministry. Despite the realization that there are those at various levels within the church who seem remarkably unaware that the interim period is "a prime time for renewal,"[3] I believe that the reality of a congregation's various manifestations of grief at the loss of a pastor is sufficient cause to move congregational leaders to embrace this emerging paradigm of parish ministry.

For Reflection and Discussion

1. Who are appropriate candidates for interim ministry?

2. How do the six distinguishing characteristics of intentional interim ministry make it different from long-term pastoral ministry?

3. What leadership qualities are important for intentional interim ministers to possess?

4. What issues are common to most congregations at the time of a pastoral transition?

5. Is it important for intentional interim ministers to have special training? Why?

PART 2

The Interim Journey

CHAPTER 6

Coming to Terms with History

Bonnie Bardot

Chuck Merritt held out a thick packet of papers and said, "You better read this before you decide whether you want to come and be our interim minister."

With that grim warning, he handed me the report of the conflict consultant hired to help the Greenville Church discover why they were beginning a search for a new pastor for the third time in six years. I took the packet from Chuck and wondered what stories I would find in the report and in the church.

Every congregation has stories to tell, stories of success and failure, stories of joy and grief. One of the times when a congregation's stories are most likely to be recalled is during the time of pastoral transition. As a congregation makes decisions for the future, members look to the past.

An interim minister can be an ideal person to help a congregation review its history. When a congregation recalls its history to celebrate an anniversary, the stories generally emphasize the success and joy. They avoid the failure and grief that are nonetheless a part of their history and have equal influence in shaping who they are today and how they will make decisions for tomorrow. The interim period is a time to celebrate a congregation's success and joy, but also a time, if the members are willing, to deal with painful stories from the recent or distant past that haunt a congregation and keep it from functioning at its best.

Telling the Congregation's Story

Who doesn't love a good story? From campfire to dinner table, people
have been instructed, initiated, and entertained through stories. Jesus
told stories to teach some of his most memorable lessons. Anyone who
has ever been part of a congregation has heard stories. Trustees tell
stories about the capital campaign for the building renovation. Church
school teachers tell stories about the superintendent who used to play
the piano for the children's worship. Deacons tell stories about faithful
church members and their years of service. These are the stories we tell
to remind ourselves of our glorious past and to inspire each other toward
a glorious future. They are stories we tell in public and they hearken
back to the good old days.

In every congregation there are other stories, stories that are told in
private, if they are told at all. Trustees might make vague references to
something strange that happened with certain funds. Older parents might
mention the incident that took place when their children were in the
youth group. Children of longtime members might be aware that their
parents still talk about something unpleasant that took place years ago.
But these stories are all in the past and have nothing to do with who we
are today. Or so we think.

During Ellen Stone's exit interview with Prairie Church, she noted
that some members of the church seemed suspicious of her with regard
to the topic of church funds. Since Ellen had given no cause for the suspicion, she suspected there was a secret in the church's history about a
previous pastor and money. Longtime members who read the report of
the exit interview were quick to acknowledge that a minister many years
ago had indeed played fast and loose with the discretionary fund. But it
was not a secret, they said, because everyone knew about it.

Stories like this one, even though everyone knows about them, still
function like secrets in the life of the church. At Prairie Church the offending minister left the church without the trustees ever raising their
concerns. The trustees were relieved not to have to deal with the un-
pleasantness, and hoping to avoid future problems, some of them quietly
took on the mission to ensure that the same thing never happened again.
As a result, subsequent ministers were viewed with suspicion. No one
ever talked about the secret. And although the trustees were relieved to
leave the past behind them, the secret prevented the minister and trustees

from ever developing genuine trust. An incident from the church's history prevented the congregation from functioning at its best and would continue to get in the way until the trustees looked at their misplaced suspicions and stopped treating their ministers with distrust.

In this case, Ellen Stone's comment in her exit interview brought the situation to light. The trustees and interim minister talked about it together and used the interim time to establish a trusting relationship between minister and church, with the trustees leading the way for the rest of the congregation. This story of past financial indiscretions, although not pleasant, was brought to light and resolved without emotional upheaval or conflict. The offense was relatively minor, the incident had occurred 15 years ago, and the principal players were no longer involved with the church. Many of our stories, however, are more painful to tell and more difficult to resolve because offenses are major, incidents are recent or ongoing, and the people involved are active members who are facing each other at worship, church meetings, and social gatherings.

The story that slowly emerged at the Corkham Congregational Church was one of widespread sexual misconduct. It appeared that the pastor was sexually involved with several women, some married and some single, for either brief or extended periods. The story was especially difficult to tell because no one would come forward with facts. A few of the deacons had bits and pieces of rumors, but when they confronted the pastor, he claimed that women in the church found him irresistible and, as hard as he tried, he couldn't keep them away. He acknowledged that the situation created rumors that made him look bad, but he denied any wrongdoing and said that he could see no reason to resign. The deacons heard more rumors, and when they again confronted the pastor, he still denied wrongdoing. This time he agreed to resign, but he made it clear to his supporters that the deacons had forced his resignation, based only on rumors.

The pastor left the church immediately but continued to date a woman who was on the church council. Among church leaders, everyone was angry. The pastor's supporters were angry at the deacons and claimed an injustice had been done because their pastor was forced to resign with no evidence of wrongdoing. The pastor's detractors were angry because none of the women had come forward with factual accusations, and therefore an injustice had been done because a potentially harmful pastor escaped disciplinary action.

Subsequently, a denominational review board conducted an investigation during which some of the women were willing to tell their stories in strict confidence. The review board gathered enough evidence to revoke the pastor's ministerial credentials, but because of the promise of confidentiality, the women's stories could not be told to the congregation.

During the interim time, church leaders and the interim minister tried to find ways to tell the story so the congregation might begin coming to terms with the truth. They could find no way to discuss the situation without either revealing the names of women who had been involved or starting rumors about those who hadn't. In some situations there is no immediate resolution. Ten years had passed, but this congregation still felt some of the hurtful effects of their unresolved history. Many members, including most of the women who were involved, have left the church. Many new people have joined. But the situation is still too recent in many people's minds for them to talk about it honestly. In rare cases it is only the passing of time that will allow honest, healing conversations to take place. For the Corkham Congregational Church, not enough time has passed.

Contrast the situation in Corkham with what happened at St. Peter's Church in Brinville. The entire congregation, including the senior pastor and the rest of the staff, learned from the evening news on TV that their associate pastor was arrested for molesting two boys who lived next door to him. For almost a year the associate pastor denied the charges, but people in the congregation were not strangled by secrets or led astray by rumors. Church leaders organized forums led by trained counselors and invited members to express everything from anger to betrayal to fear. People who held sharply different opinions were encouraged to express them to each other in a civilized forum. People who disagreed passionately over whether their pastor was innocent or guilty were still able to worship together and pray for him and his family, and for the two boys.

When the associate pastor admitted his guilt a year later, members of the church received the news with sadness, but without bitterness toward each other. Although it was a terrible shock for church members to hear the news about their associate pastor's arrest on TV, the public disclosure ensured that the matter would be discussed openly and not become a divisive church secret. It is always easier to keep our secrets hidden and hope that they will go away, but they almost never do. Most churches don't have TV cameras bringing their stories to light; rather, if secrets are going to be brought out and exorcised, the members must do the work themselves.

The interim time is ideal for carrying out this work, and the interim minister is the ideal person to help the congregation with these sensitive tasks. Although interim ministers quickly come to know and love each congregation, they have no personal investment in how stories are told about the past or in how information will be used to shape the future. They can help a congregation to tell their stories, they can lead the congregation in hearing the difference between helpful facts and hurtful fiction, and they can guide a congregation in using that information to plan for its future. The stories have nothing to do with them personally, so they can focus their attention on the congregation without being distracted. In addition, when interim ministers have completed their work with a congregation, they leave. Some church members feel more at ease speaking their minds to an interim minister. They know that when the congregation is ready to move forward, it will be with a new pastoral leader who has not witnessed the harsh words and actions that often are a part of hearing stories and resolving the conflict that surrounds them.

James Lane Allen expressed this idea eloquently in his Victorian novel, *The Mettle of the Pasture*, when he observed:

> "Among a primitive folk . . . there grew up the custom of using a curious expedient. They chose a beast of the field and upon its head symbolically piled all the moral hardheadedness of the several tribes; after which the unoffending brute was banished to the wilderness and the guilty multitude felt relieved. However crude that ancient method of transferring mental and moral burdens, it had at least this redeeming feature: the early Hebrews heaped their sins upon a creature which they did not care for and sent it away. In modern times we pile our burdens upon our dearest fellow-creatures and keep them permanently near us for further use."[1]

Interim ministers generally are not viewed by our congregations as "creatures which they did not care for," and they can't relieve a congregation's pain by simply carrying it away. But once they have helped a congregation struggle with hurtful chapters of its history, they can symbolically carry away residual burdens, making them less accessible for further use. Your interim minister will help members of your congregation to hear your stories. Story telling and listening times might take place formally or informally, or both. They might be planned for committee meetings, small groups, or all-church potluck suppers. Depending upon the particular circumstances of your congregation, your interim minister will lead you in using your stories to celebrate your successes and learn from your failures.

Dealing with Grief

If there is one unifying characteristic experienced by every congregation during the interim time, it is grief. At least some of the members of every congregation will feel grief about saying goodbye to a pastor, no matter what circumstances might surround the pastor's leaving. Even if a pastor has managed to offend everyone in the congregation, some members will still grieve for the hopes that were never realized and the promises that were never fulfilled.

When Paul Broderick left Brighton Church, even the people who personally liked him had to admit that his dull sermons and seeming lack of interest in the church would not be missed; but they still mourned the fact that the enthusiasm of his first year had suddenly disappeared and never come back. In this instance, grief for some people was expressed more as guilt—for causing their minister to get bored and leave. Others just blamed themselves for calling a minister who was not a good choice. The time of mourning at the Brighton Church was brief—a matter of people acknowledging that Pastor Broderick was not the right minister for them, wishing him well in his next call, and preparing to move on.

At the Oldfield Church, Charles O'Neill retired after 32 years. During his pastorate he baptized, confirmed, married, and buried hundreds in his active congregation and enjoyed an affectionate pastoral relationship with most of the church. While people made plans to celebrate his retirement, they still felt a terrible loss at his leaving. Since Charles stayed in town after he retired, some of the sense of loss came from hurt feelings and confusion over why he wouldn't come back to participate in baptisms and weddings. After all, he had officiated at all the family events for the past 32 years and he really knew the families well.

During the interim time, members of the Oldfield Church had to face their grief, understand that their retired pastor was no longer available to carry out pastoral duties, and accept a new relationship with him. The interim minister helped the congregation to remember that Charles had not known them when he first arrived at their church. He had come to know them as he celebrated their sacred events, and their new minister needed the chance to do the same.

Sometimes a congregation and a retired minister need reminders as they define and grow into new roles with each other. The interim minister can help a former minister deal with requests from church members and can help church members to resist making requests of the former minister. At first, even gentle reminders may upset people who aren't ready to let go of their retired minister. In time, however, most people realize how important it is for them to do just that if they are to wholeheartedly welcome their new minister. An interim minister can be of particular service by working through this transition with the congregation, especially so that hard feelings and misunderstandings can be resolved before the new minister arrives.

When a minister leaves a church in the midst of conflict, the grief is even more complex. At Center Church, after seven years of controversial ministry, Jack Benton left behind such well-defined conflict that the two opposing groups had names. The Groupies, who supported Jack and his innovative ideas, were devastated when he accepted another call. They felt not only grief because of his leaving, but also anger because of the way he had been treated by the Opponents. Members of the Opponents were angry at the Groupies who had insulted anyone who opposed Jack, and they were devastated because many friends had withdrawn their church membership in protest. Several of the people who had withdrawn returned on the interim minister's first Sunday. Their presence was noted by the Opponents who welcomed them, saying how good it was to have them back. Their return was also noted by the Groupies, who observed that they better not think they could just come back and run the church.

Grief, complicated by anger, paralyzed most of the leaders of the church. Both sides were determined to have the upper hand during the interim time and in the search for a new minister. Both sides tried to be the first to plead its case to the interim minister. Both sides had legitimate complaints about each other. But beneath all the bitterness, there were people on opposing sides who had known each other for years and who had worked together to serve their church and their community. Although now pitted against each other, these people often had comforted each other in tragedy and had encouraged each other through hard times.

Healing began when a woman from the Opponents mentioned to the interim minister how much she missed some of the Groupies, especially one woman who had offered help and support when the Opponent's son was ill. The two women, who each had credibility in their respective groups, agreed to meet together with the interim minister over coffee and listen to each other. The meeting began with prayer, and each woman expressed her opinions and concerns about the church conflict. After the meeting the women agreed to meet again and also agreed that the interim minister could tell the congregation that they had met. Details of their conversations were kept confidential, but just the fact that the women were talking together was enough to break the ice. There was no spontaneous reconciliation, but there was the beginning of communication and a gradual willingness to work together again.

Celebrating Our Strengths

Some church members have confessed to me that they thought an interim minister was someone who would come in and tell them everything that was wrong with their church. It might have felt that way to Chuck Merritt when he handed me the conflict consultant's report on the Greenville Church. After two brief pastorates in six years and long searches between, the people in Greenville didn't think there was anything positive to be found in their church. Indeed, the consultant's report did point out some serious problems, but the report itself was evidence that the members were willing to take a hard look at themselves and presumably they were also willing to make some changes. Because so many people were discouraged, the first thing we did was to make a pact that we would continue to be the church together, no matter what. Having done that, we set aside the report for a month while we celebrated Advent and got to know each other.

What emerged in the Greenville Church was a solid group of people who cared passionately for their church and their small town. Many were longtime members with strong opinions about the right way to go about the church's business. Among the church's strengths was a considerable endowment; among its weaknesses was a group of trustees reluctant to spend any of it.

As we studied the consultant's report together, we found a common thread that had to do with money. The minister's salary was very low, there were serious problems with the parsonage, and many people didn't support the church financially because the church already had lots of money that it didn't use. Two things the church had to do were to stop hoarding its money and to start being fair about the pastor's compensation. The congregation began to understand that they are people with strong opinions and strong personalities. They needed a pastor with the skills and maturity to provide strong leadership, and they needed to offer a better compensation package to attract someone with the necessary experience. (In fact, this subject was initially raised with the interim search committee at my interview when I said that I would love to accept their call, but I couldn't afford to be their interim minister at the level of compensation they were offering. The search committee and I determined a fair package and the church council approved it.) In times of crisis, a congregation forgets to celebrate its strengths, and the time of pastoral transition is perceived as at least a minor crisis in most congregations. When the transition is accompanied by conflict, the sense of crisis becomes more pronounced and it becomes even more important to help the congregation to remember to celebrate their strengths. One of the most joyful tasks of interim ministry is helping people recognize and celebrate their strengths as a community of faith.

For Reflection and Discussion

1. Are there stories in your church that you wouldn't tell a new member? Why not?

2. If there is conflict in your church, what is one positive thing you could say about people who hold an opinion opposite yours? What is one positive thing they could say about you?

3. Think about some people who have been active members of your church for many years. What has kept them active and involved?

4. What excites you about your church?

CHAPTER 7

Discovering a New Identity

Linda Lea Snyder

To begin the task of discovering a new identity, think back to an occasion of Jesus praying alone.

His disciples draw near and Jesus asks them, "Who do the crowds say that I am?"

The disciples set forth an array of answers: John the Baptist, Elijah, an ancient prophet from the past. Jesus probes for their personal response.

"But who do you say that I am?" he asks.

And Peter, boldly and clearly, proclaims, "The Messiah of God" (Luke 9:18-20).

In so many ways the world is asking the church today, "Who do *you* say that you are?" The interim time is an ideal time to boldly consider what your answer to this question might be.

You Are a New Creature

One of the firmest foundations of our Christian faith is that we worship a God who, in Christ, is continually "doing a new thing." We think of Paul's central teaching on this act of God's continual regeneration. He sets it forth to the Corinthians: "So if anyone is in Christ, there is a new creation: everything old has passed away; see, everything has become new!" (2 Cor. 5:17) Day by day and year by year, in seed-like fashion, this new realm Jesus talked about is coming into existence before our very eyes. Paul writes to the church at Rome that the whole creation longs for this new thing like a woman longing for the birth of her child. We are being made new as individual believers and as communities of faith. We are dying to the old and being born to the new. As this new-ness breaks forth, we are invited by God to be co-creators and midwives with God and to recognize and name these new things. By doing so, we receive and claim a new identity.

A Closer Look at This New Identity

Our identities change through the years. Personally speaking, it always takes me a while to catch up with my current identity. Just the other week I found myself saying by phone to a washing-machine repairperson that I needed immediate service because I am the mother of three young children. The fact of the matter is that my children are all in middle and senior high school. I was appealing to his sympathy, of course. I needed my washing machine fixed pronto. And the "house-full-of-dirty-laundry-with-small-children-clinging-to-my-knee" picture might just elicit sym-pathy for a quick service call! But the identity I conveyed was not a *true* identity. The true picture is that any one of my children is capable of doing laundry. They could go by themselves to the laundromat down the street and wash and dry their own clothes. My oldest could even drive to the laundromat. It only took me a mental second to be conscious of the fact that I am definitely not the mother of young children anymore. But the new picture—the new thing God is doing—is not fully formed in my heart or psyche yet. Even as I spoke to this repairperson, I could see I had it wrong. A moment of reflection enabled an "aha" experience. There was a gap between my perceived identity and my true identity.

When a congregation experiences the departure of their pastor or other staff person, they will often begin to recognize that through the years the identity of the congregation has changed, either a little or a great deal. It is not uncommon for the congregation to recognize during the interim that part of their identity rested on their former pastor's per-sonality, style, or spiritual gifts. The interim time gives freedom to ex-amine who they are apart from the influence of their pastor's identity. In making any of these discoveries, they may come to see that their con-gregation has not yet caught up emotionally, spiritually, or behaviorally with those changes. As it was for me as my children grew, the perceived identity may be out of sync with what is true and real.

What Is Identity?

When we talk about identity, what are we talking about? First, it is the way we understand ourselves. This includes how we think of ourselves and how we describe ourselves to others. Reflect on all the ways we characterize our congregations. We say, for example, that we are friendly or are concerned about mission. We often identify ourselves by our programs or ministries or staff or gifts. We might know who we are by how we spend our money or time, by how big we are, or by how we worship together. Even the things we hope for shape our identities. We ask small children what they want to be when they grow up because those visions tell us something about who that child is today. So our hopes for the future, our experience from the past, and our present realities all combine to form our identity.

Sizing Up Our Current Perceptions

A task squarely before you during the interim time is to become conscious of who you are. Yes, you are a congregation and share a thousand characteristics with other congregations. But certain things make your identity unique. If a new neighbor were to approach you looking for a church home, what are some of the characteristics of your congregation you would share? The way in which you use words to describe yourselves paints a picture of how *you* see your identity. Because outsiders or newcomers can often see in us what we cannot see, it is important to ask for input beyond ourselves. Surveying neighbors—other churches in town or groups that use our building—for their "take" on us can provide a useful perspective.[1]

Questions related to this task of discovering a new identity are: Do perceptions of ourselves—our perceived identity—match reality? In what ways has reality changed since the last time we looked? Since the world does not stand still, how has our context (the neighborhood or our world) changed? How have we as a congregation changed? What spiritual gifts are present in our congregation today? In light of these contextual and spiritual gift changes, what is God calling us to be or do as a community of faith? Answers to these questions will point to a reality-based identity for your congregation and go a long way toward helping you to recognize and call a good match in your next pastor.

Vocation

As my son begins to think seriously about college, his dad and I talk to
him about his unique skills and gifts. But these alone do not point the
way to a possible career choice. As people of faith, we also try to talk
to him about the great needs of the world. We believe faithfulness and
blessing lie in discerning that place where his particular gifts and the
needs around him intersect. This discernment work is the work of discovering vocation. So it is for us as churches. This task of discovering
a new identity is related to discovering your true vocation, that is, that
place where one's unique gifts and the world's great needs intersect.[2]

Why the Resistance?

Many congregations experience some resistance to this work. Most of
us—thank you—are comfortable with our tried-and-true old identity.
For better or worse, how I describe and think of myself are just fine the
way they are. Considering a new identity can be threatening. It may go
to the very heart of who I believe myself to be. Further, considering a
new identity may imply that my "old" identity was somehow faulty. My
reluctance to look at new realities also has something to do with my not
paying attention. Given the fast pace of life, we can't always monitor
the change meter. And, although some change is fast-paced, most changes
happen gradually, almost undetectably. Even when you notice something different, acknowledging it can be difficult because it means
heart-wrenchingly letting go of an old identity.

Let's go back to my experience with the washer repairperson. If,
indeed, my children are not babies anymore, that must mean that other
things have changed as well. For example, acknowledging that my children are older must mean *I am older*. It may further mean that I am not
needed in quite the same ways by my children (they can do their own
wash!). It's just a matter of time—I think with some horror—that I will
be eased out of this job of mothering altogether! Acknowledging and
naming one new reality can start in motion a whole series of new reve-
lations, some of which can be downright scary to think about.

Our commitment to stay with the quest can be grounded in faith.
Jesus' great teaching that when we "continue in his word we will know

the truth and the truth will make us free" (John 8:31-32) is a promise that can fill us with courage as we grieve for things we are leaving behind.

Discovering and claiming a new identity not only ground us in reality (usually a good thing), but they also open up to us possibilities inherent in that newness. Embracing my own changing identity allowed me to celebrate my children being able to do their own laundry and being able to drive.

After we've sized up our present identity by looking around, listening to each other, and asking outsiders for feedback, we are ready to measure these new findings over and against the context in which we find ourselves.

A Fresh Look at Context

There are many instruments and strategies that will enable you to get an accurate picture of your context today. First, get a handle on your church's context. What's going on in your own neighborhood? What has changed? What has stayed the same? Try not to complain that things aren't as good as they used to be. Remember, God is doing a new thing, not the same old thing again. And whatever's going on is your context for ministry!

Consider these means of gathering data about your context:

- Many national denominational offices provide services related to demographic studies of the geographic area in which your congregation is located.[3] Your local government's planning board or your Chamber of Commerce can also generate such information for you.
- Another approach is to send out representatives from the congregation (alone, or in twos for double the listening power) to interview various members of the community—the school principal, a local store owner, someone from social services, or political leaders. Together these community folks can tell you how they see things. Go forth with the mission of discovering what the needs of the community are and how those needs are being met or not being met.[4] Keep an eye open for potential future partnerships between church and community that could meet those needs.

- Another way of tuning into your neighborhood is to take a stroll around the neighborhood. Keep your eyes and ears open. What do you see or hear? Are houses and buildings in good repair? Are there children out playing? What language or languages are people speaking? What is the feeling of the neighborhood? Is it tense? Is it a place apart? Are there teenagers around? What pastimes are people engaged in? Are they riding bikes or standing around? Are there dangers or needs that you quickly pick up on? Or are they more subtle and hidden?

- Another strategy is to visit other congregations in small teams. Call ahead if it seems necessary. At an appropriate moment introduce yourself. Return to your home base and, over a cup of soup or a slice of pizza, share your insights regarding what you've learned about your context through this experience.

- Another successful strategy can be to host a potluck meal or dessert time and invite your neighbors in. Have members of the congregation bring one or more people to tell "how they see the neighborhood." Tell them they are doing you a favor and that anything goes. Tack up a large sheet of newsprint so that you can record people's input.

- Develop a one-page questionnaire and conduct a formal survey door to door. Have on hand a brochure describing your church and ask to conduct the survey orally while you are there. Another approach might be to stand on a corner of the neighborhood (in twos or threes) and ask for similar input from passersby. Be good-natured and of good cheer.

- Consider an Open Forum Sunday School.[5] Each Sunday invite a community leader, such as an attorney, to talk with an adult class about issues he or she faces. Someone in the class records what your guest has to say. On the following Sunday, the class reflects on how the congregation might respond to the issues that were lifted up. The following week you might invite a local social worker, and so forth. Ask these leaders what they are dealing with in the course of their work and their opinion on community needs and changes.

All these strategies will give you official input. You will also receive informal input and "mirroring back." Your interim minister may say things in worship, or newcomers might reflect on what attracted them to your church. Though you will not choose to act on all this input, keep your ears open for this unofficial information. It can be the most telling of all.

The overall quest is to be in touch with your community. Remember, whatever process you choose for being in touch, make it a congregational process. The more folks you involve at this assessment stage, the more ownership there will be later. After each walk, or each visit, or each interview with a community leader, do not forget to record your findings for your own recollections. New information, especially if it goes against the grain of our preconceptions, can be easily forgotten. Writing it down will enable you to share the information later with the whole congregation.

The Wider Community

Now that you feel you have some idea of how your immediate context has changed, it is time to look more closely at the wider context, specifically the national scene. Many church sociologists are writing about changes in American life—how they are reflected in people's changing habits and behavior and how they impact the church. It is important that your committee is up to speed on these changes.

One congregation with whom I work has a wonderful and growing church school program. With the renewal this congregation has experienced, the whole ministry of Christian education has been reworked as a result of changes in their context. For example, the high mobility and transience of folks in their neighborhood has impacted how they ask for teaching commitments from prospective teachers. Many of the newer members are attached to the local university and will be part of the church for only three to five years. Much of the numerical growth is due largely to families with young children. Parents are working outside the home and are likely to be engaged in some kind of academic pursuit. Other adults are working three or more jobs just to make ends meet.

In short, time is at a premium and most of the adults in the community are not in a position to commit to the traditional September-to-June year of weekly teaching. (Often they feel as if they are tacitly committing to teach from now until they retire or die!) Twelve to sixteen weeks is a more realistic commitment. These new folks also enjoy teaching in

teams of two, both for the freedom it gives them to be away occasionally, and for the companionship and synergy it offers.

Other dynamics affect the teaching ministry. Some children can be
with their classes only every other week because they move between two
households. Other children and youth are involved in the congregation
largely without the participation of the adults in their families. These
societal changes tell us of new realities and should, if we are paying
attention, impact our identity as a congregation.

There are several books and articles that talk about the changing
habits and behavior of people living in the United States today. *Congregational Megatrends* by Jeff Woods, *The Once and Future Church* by
Loren Mead, and *Congregation and Community* by Nancy Ammerman
are great primers. Mead sees the changes as dramatic enough to warrant
nothing less than reinvention of our congregations. Ammerman also
notes great changes, but talks about adapting to the changes. Whether
we embark on reinvention or adaptation, these writers and others are
telling us that the changes needed are radical. Trying to accommodate
them without newness on our part will be akin to putting new wine in
old wineskins. *All* could be lost (Matt 9:17). Consider a six-to-ten-week
adult study group using books by authors such as Mead or Woods so that
a core of the congregation will be "in the know." This core can then
pass on the word to other circles of ministry and friendship within the
congregation.

Discovering Your Spiritual Gifts

Having looked at your present perceptions of who you are (your current
identity) and how your contexts (both locally and nationally) are changing, you may now benefit from assessing your congregation itself, especially with an eye to what gifts lie with the membership of your congregation. Remember, discovering a new identity is similar to discerning
a true vocation. You are seeking to focus clearly on that point of inter-
section between your unique gifts and the world's great needs. From the
information you gathered about your context, you now know something
about the world's needs. Now you need to get clear on the unique gifts
God has given members of your particular congregation.

Research today is telling us that one way congregations experience renewal is to have each member be aware of, and using, his or her spiritual gifts. (See Ephesians 4, Romans 12, 1 Corinthians 12, and 1 Peter 4.) Engaging in ministry can no longer be left solely to paid church staff. Indeed, very few newcomers *want* to assign ministry to paid staff. Busyness and emptiness threaten the best among us. Most of us are looking to fill our time with pursuits that really matter. What could matter more than working with God to birth a new realm? Both inside the church (arranging an art show or teaching a class) or outside the church (parenting, teaching school, or volunteering at the soup kitchen), all of us, as Christians via our baptism, are called to be in ministry. Our renewal and vitality as God's people are tied up with doing so—both as individuals and as faith communities. Discovering the spiritual gifts the Holy Spirit has bestowed is the beginning of direction-finding for many congregations. So, too, embracing other kinds of skills and talents that are not listed in Scripture (such as carpentry, medical know-how, or the arts) but which are present in your congregation can aid in understanding who you are as God's people in this place and at this time. Indeed, renewal is coming to many congregations as they move from a program-based ministry to one that is broadly gift-based. Recognizing, knowing, and naming these gifts, as we've said, can go a long way in discovering your congregation's true identity.

There are many resources available today that lead a congregation through a process of gift discovery.[6] This generally is a fun process of happy confirmation or outright surprise. Whatever resource you choose, consider which format might work best for your congregation—for example, a series of six to ten once-a-week meetings or a weekend retreat with follow-up sessions. Assign the tasks of exploring resources, planning, and leadership to one of your boards or mission teams. Ask the interim pastor for input. Think about leadership. Do you want to ask your interim pastor, hire someone from the outside, or share leadership among yourselves? Ask your denominational staff if another church in your area has engaged in such a process. If so, invite them in. I have found the weekend retreat format works well intergenerationally, provided there is a separate track going for the very young children. It is important for each individual, regardless of age or circumstance, to have the opportunity to identify his or her giftedness.

One congregation for whom I led an intergenerational "Discover Your Gifts" weekend retreat (they led their own follow-up sessions) found their hunches confirmed and new gifts brought to light. Some folks identified evangelism and outreach as particular gifts. Others identified gifts in the performing arts and other artistic talents. This was a healthy congregation that was feeling stuck. These new discoveries pointed to possible new directions for ministry.

A final part of the retreat process was designed to link spiritual gifts to actual ministry. Recognizing their gifts as individuals put them onto new ideas for personal ministry; recognizing their gifts as a group enabled them to see new possibilities for the congregation as a whole. For example, they knew there were many unchurched folks within their community. This information about context, combined with new information related to their newly discovered gifts (evangelism and performing arts), had them thinking and praying about the possibilities of creating stage productions that might invite people to consider Jesus Christ as Lord and Savior.

Other "Gifts" to Uncover

"Know thyself," said the ancient sage. In-depth self-study can be very valuable.[7] In addition to spiritual gifts, there are other aspects or descriptors of your congregation that can be understood as gifts from God. You need to know what these are and be able to describe them to anyone who might ask, because the church officials helping with your pastoral search and the prospective pastoral candidates surely will ask! Knowing yourselves entails being in touch with certain factual information about your congregation that you can't gather in surveys: membership size, age/generational makeup, the tenures of the last several pastors, and the shape and condition of your physical plant. These and a thousand other descriptors help identify you. You may be described as the big church with the beautiful stained-glass windows, or the church where pastors only stay for two years. So you need to be aware of these identifying characteristics about yourselves and factor them into an assessment of your giftedness. For good or bad, you can view every piece of information about yourselves as a gift for direction-finding in ministry. Each piece of information may also help you more accurately discover your true identity.

Conclusion

This task of discovering a new identity can be one of the most exciting components of your interim time as a congregation. It is work inextricably tied to the other developmental tasks, especially the tasks of coming to terms with history and committing to new directions in ministry. Work on the other tasks will also be work on this one. Bit by bit, when you develop an eye for it, you will begin to see the outlines of a new identity that God is giving you for the next chapter of your journey as a community of faith. In that identity you will find your greatest clarity of mission and your fullest joy as a congregation. Knowing yourselves will also help you make a good leadership match in your next pastor.

For Reflection and Discussion

1. Think of a time in your personal life when you resisted moving into a new identity. Discuss the points of resistance and the ways you believe they were overcome.

2. What are some of the words you use to describe your congregation to would-be newcomers? Brainstorm words that describe your hopes for how your congregation might be in the future.

3. Name some of the "new things" God is bringing to life in your congregation. In what ways might these be pointing to a new vocation?

4. What changes have you noticed in your life (the culture?) that affect our congregations? What do you appreciate about how your congregation has sought to honor these changes?

5. Now that your pastor or other staff person is no longer with you, what changes have you noticed in the way your congregation lives out its life? What losses are people grieving? What new possibilities have been created that didn't exist as fully before?

6. How does this task of Discovering a New Identity fit together with your other work on the developmental tasks? Which task sparks your imagination as being most critical to accomplishing the work set forth in this chapter?

CHAPTER 8

Leadership Changes during an Interim

Andrew E. Carlsson

There appears to be a crisis in leadership today. This may be an understatement! There is an apparent crisis in leadership in the national and international scene. We are experiencing this crisis in local organizations as well. We have come to distrust our leaders. We sometimes wonder why we even have leaders. Let's do away with leaders!

The story is told of a group of Christians who decided to start a new church. They were offered the use of a small barn on land belonging to one person in the group. They renovated the space and began to gather for worship on Sundays. They decided not to have leaders, and they certainly did not want any committees. This lasted for a few months, and then chaos, confusion, arguments, power plays, hurt feelings, and a host of other issues began to develop.

The church, like any human organization, needs structure and process. The church, like any organism, will develop structure and process. Leaders will surface in every community, including the local congregation, often called the "faith community." There may be regular and normal changes in the leadership; however, there are certain times in community life when such change is likely to intensify and even develop into power struggles. The roles and functions of leaders may also shift. One such time for congregations is definitely during pastoral transition, the interim between installed pastors. Let me illustrate this with a couple of scenarios that I experienced as an interim pastor.

Scenario 1: Community Church

Nothing was said during my initial interviews with Community Church about the need for leadership and staff changes. I had two productive meetings with the council, and also a breakfast meeting with the former pastor of over 30 years. I didn't sense any significant leadership problems. Little did I know!

I began a one-year interim ministry with Community Church on July 1. I arrived at the office somewhat early and unpacked my "first-aid" kit for interim ministry. At about 9:15 A.M. it dawned on me that Carol, the office secretary, had not yet come in. She was part-time and had worked at Community Church in the mornings for the past two years. The time went by, and no office secretary arrived.

It was Wednesday, so I began to gather material for the Sunday bulletin. I called the lay leader, Bob, who said he did not know why the secretary wasn't there, but he would give her a call. A few minutes later Bob called back to say there was no answer at Carol's house. Noon came and went, but no office secretary appeared that day.

Thursday morning I returned to the church office, and again by noon there was no office secretary. Telephone calls were made to her, but there was no answer. On Friday morning I talked with Bob again. We discussed the need for a Sunday worship bulletin and other secretarial tasks that needed to be done. Another lay leader, Aretha, told me that her sister worked as office secretary for the Presbyterian church in town, and maybe she would do the bulletin for us. Indeed, she agreed to help us. However, by the end of the day there was still no word from the office secretary of Community Church.

On Wednesday of the next week, Bob called me to say that the night before, while he was at the church office, Carol had come in. She told him that she had taken another job and had come to pick up her things. We would have to look for another office secretary. I asked myself, "Is this what they meant at interim ministry training by leadership change?!" Carol's departure was only the beginning.

The next day Bob called to tell me that the choir director, Mae, had sent him a letter giving her resignation, effective "as soon as you find another director." One week later the janitor, Tom, submitted his resignation, effective the end of the month.

At my next meeting with Bob he told me, "I have another bit of information. Louise, the council secretary, has just resigned."

The words kept going through my head: "During a pastoral transition there will be many leadership changes." In training we were told that one of the developmental tasks for the congregation during an interim was to deal with "power shifts" as leadership changed. Yes, indeed!

Scenario 2: Advent Church

In another congregation, Advent Church, the leadership change was more "normal." The former pastor had resigned under pressure and accepted a call to another congregation. Advent Church was divided over his leaving. Sally, the janitor, resigned immediately. The office secretary, Cheryl, gave two weeks' notice, and Ann, the treasurer, resigned.

During my initial interview with the church council I could see it coming. Two council members, Dolly and Sam, resigned at the meeting. The next month Charles, the president of the council, resigned. Leadership change! Again!

I now anticipate this change after having served more than 15 interim congregations. During a pastoral transition there are going to be shifts of power and leadership changes. Some of these changes will involve paid staff; others will occur with elected or volunteer leaders.

Members of the congregation will have various responses and reactions to this leadership change. Some will feel that the ship is going down. I call it the "Titanic syndrome." A few members will have difficulty handling the anxiety that comes with the loss of leadership and staff. Others will feel disappointment and betrayal from those leaving the ship in its time of need. A few members might even blame the new interim pastor. Some parishioners may express feelings of guilt over such leadership changes, wondering what they did to cause such changes. Other members may express anger about all the turmoil.

As I reflected on the congregations I have served, especially these two situations, I discovered several reasons for the change in leadership during a pastoral vacancy. Certainly there had been changes in leadership and/or shifts in power many times during the former pastor's tenure, but congregational systems seem to be more prone to these changes during a pastoral transition. There is often a variety of factors in play when leadership changes occur at this time.

Some leaders bail out because they have been enmeshed in the past. I discovered later that Carol, at Community Church, had been loyal to the former pastor and had apparently taken on the job as a favor to him. She now felt that she was no longer needed and sought a better-paying job. The janitor, Tom, had not liked the hours, especially with Saturday weddings. He was also tired of all the complaints. Now he saw an opportunity to get out. Mae, the choir director, was a personal friend of the retired pastor. She felt that the pastor had many years left for ministry, but that the power structure had pushed him out. Mae was sure no pastor could replace him, especially a "fill-in" like me. She felt it was now time to leave. Louise had held the job of council secretary for 20 years and was tired of doing all the work. She had stayed with the task primarily out of loyalty to the former pastor. This leadership change should have come as no surprise to the members of Community Church, but it did!

At Advent Church Sally and Ann were both upset about the way the members had treated the pastor, and they blamed the council for "getting rid of him." Dolly and Sam blamed each other for the loss of the pastor. Ann thought it was great that he left; he deserved better than the treatment he had been getting at Advent Church. Some council members even wondered if Ann might have "fixed" the books in order to give the pastor a $500 farewell check. Charles simply said, "I've had enough!"

As we seek to better understand the interim time in a congregation, one of the questions we need to ask is, "Why does leadership change so quickly and so often at the time of pastoral transition?" Let's consider some answers to this question.

Reasons for Leadership Change

We can see from the stories of Community Church and Advent Church that some members took sides and then found themselves caught in a conflict. Some had supported the former pastor while others had been critical of him. Either way, they got caught in the middle, and some of them figured that the thing to do was "to get out." That's what appeared to happen with Mae at Community Church. Her loyalty to the former pastor was so personal and strong that she felt his departure was the result of a strategy by the power structure of the congregation. People frequently attach themselves to pastors and often become leaders working closely with their pastor. When the pastor leaves, strong feelings begin to surface and may be expressed in the ways that Mae and others did.

At Advent Church Sally, Cheryl, and Ann seemed to be caught in the middle of such a controversy. They blamed the board for "getting rid of our pastor." The blaming game had perhaps begun several months prior to the resignation of the pastor. Everywhere they turned they found themselves defending the pastor. Each of them felt she had to resign in order to demonstrate her loyalty to the former pastor, as well as to "save face."

Mae at Community Church and several people at Advent Church expressed grief over the loss of their pastor. They tended to see the former pastor's style as the only way to lead. The absence of their former pastor on Sunday was a reminder of the loss of his ministry and friendship. Even the presence of the interim pastor did not immediately take away that grief.

Tom and Louise at Community Church were tired of their tasks and perhaps suffered from burnout. They needed to get out. No doubt this was also true for Charles, and perhaps for Dolly and Sam at Advent Church. It is often the case that some people have been at their tasks in the congregation too long. They may have perceived a lack of support from the other leaders. Tom may have felt that he was being taken for granted in his tasks and that the former pastor was the only one who gave him the strokes he needed to continue his work. With that support now gone, Tom saw his chance to leave.

These stories and examples of leadership change are not unique. I have witnessed them in almost every congregation I have served as an intentional interim pastor. Whenever there is pastoral change, no matter the size of the congregation, there will be changes in the leadership and in the power structure of that congregation.

At the time of pastoral transition there are often signs that leadership issues have not been resolved. A lot of blaming goes on in these situations. There may be power plays, competition, and divisions. There may be hurt feelings, gossip, and rumors. Sometimes the issues become so divisive that secret meetings are held and win-lose decisions are urged. Needless to say, this climate is not conducive to securing a new pastor. Even though we may think that the new pastor will change things, he or she may become the focus for unresolved issues, straining the pastoral relationship before it even begins.

How to Deal with Change

What can a congregation in pastoral transition do about changes in leadership as it begins to prepare for the future with a new pastor? Hopefully, the congregation will seek support and insight from the intentional interim minister. When there are leadership and staff changes in a congregation, the interim specialist will work with the congregation on four very clear and specific tasks.

Attend to Former Leaders

First of all, with the assistance of the interim pastor you will help departing leaders be clear in their own minds about their leaving. They may need help to understand why they desire to step down from their positions. Feelings of blame, guilt, anger, and betrayal need to be dealt with. It is unfortunate, but often happens, that these former leaders will even separate themselves from the congregation. Nevertheless, as the current congregational leaders, you will need to support these former leaders and convey to them your understanding of their feelings and decisions. Furthermore, it is neither helpful to them nor to the congregation to attempt to unduly persuade them to return to the leadership circle or even to congregational participation.

Accept and Deal with Change

Second, let the interim minister help your congregation understand and deal with the reality that leadership changes and power shifts usually occur during a pastoral transition. It really does happen all the time! Your congregation will not sink!

Many of these leadership changes will come in the first few months of the pastoral transition. Some changes may even occur before the interim pastor begins her or his ministry. It is important that the other leaders and the members of the congregation do not panic when these changes occur. Rather, this is the time to examine leadership needs and the gifts that your members bring to the congregation. Your immediate concern may well be the kind of leadership needed during this interim period. You may want to elect a steering committee to guide your congregation in this transition process.

It is also important to be thinking about what kind of leadership the congregation will need following the interim time. By using the Myers-Briggs Type Indicator or a leadership-style analysis tool, you can discover important information about your present leadership. A well-balanced leadership group will have many different, and sometimes opposing, styles. As Max DePree notes in his book *Leadership Is An Art*, a congregation's leadership is like an organ or a choir. There are many different kinds of voices, but when integrated, they make up a wonderful musical expression.

Focus on the Mission

A third task for the congregation during leadership change is to focus on the congregation's mission. When we are preoccupied with our weaknesses or problems, we tend to forget what our real purpose is. During the interim time, the congregation has five developmental tasks. If you become immobilized about the leadership changes that are occurring, you may have difficulty working on the other important tasks.

One way to prevent the congregation from becoming immobilized is to celebrate the ministry of former leaders, including those who left under less than desirable circumstances. This may also help the congregation deal with the past. It is appropriate to recognize the work of former leaders. We need to honor the skills, knowledge, and contributions of our people. Former leaders can even be used as mentors to the rising new leadership. The first six months after the pastoral transition may be an opportune time to recognize and celebrate retiring leaders. A dinner, picnic, or liturgical expression in worship might be planned to recognize members who served as leaders. Such recognition can help to bring closure to the leadership of the past.

Another way to help the congregation focus on its mission is to review and clarify all personnel policies, descriptions, and procedures, and to determine if they support the congregation's mission. If they do not, you need to discover what needs to be changed so that they reflect that mission. The question of "Whose job is it?" occurs frequently in congregational life. It is important to obtain clarity in task descriptions, and this can be accomplished without lengthy detail.

I once accompanied an interim pastor to a large congregation one Sunday morning. He indicated that he needed to be at the church an hour before the eight o'clock liturgy. I wondered why, and Sunday morning I found out! He had to unlock all the doors, turn on the lights, and check that the thermostats were adjusted correctly.

"Don't they have a custodian here?" I asked.

"Yes, but he doesn't like to work on Sunday mornings!"

I suggested that a review of leadership tasks was in order!

Seek Out New Leaders

Finding new leaders may not be an easy task. After all, the anxiety in the congregation is quite high during the interim, and some members may not want to get involved. On the other hand, there may be a few members who want to come in and "straighten things out." This is an opportunity to seek out people with gifts, skills, and a desire to serve in the congregation.

New leaders may include those who had been overlooked during the former pastor's time. Perhaps there are some who just didn't "fit in" with the previous pastor. It is also possible that the interim minister's style will attract some people for leadership positions. It is important that these new leaders be trained in their ministry. A workshop about leadership development will be important in this process. Your interim pastor may do this or help you to find a resource for such training.

A Systemic Look at Leadership

As we struggle to understand and deal with leadership changes during a pastoral transition, it is important to remember that the congregation is an emotional system. (See chapter 3, "The Church in Transition as a Human System.") Carol, Tom, Mae, Bob, and Louise were part of a congregational system known as Community Church. Sally, Cheryl, Ann, Dolly, Sam, and Charles were also part of a congregational system, a system known as Advent Church. Why did the departure of the pastors of Community Church and Advent Church cause so much reaction? After all, hundreds of pastors leave or retire from congregations every day. People retire from schools, industry, small businesses, offices, and a host of other situations. Are there similar reactions to these changes in leadership in other organizations? On the surface it appears that there are. However, a congregation is uniquely different. A congregation is a unique, emotional system.

Biblical images that can be used to describe this reality include the people of God, Israel, the body of Christ, and the shepherd and flock, as well as the church. The church is not simply an organization of individuals who have similar thoughts, ideas, and religious expressions. These individuals are emotionally bound together. Leaders of the congregation have an emotional relationship with all of the members, and all of the members have an emotional relationship with the leaders.

Each individual leader has adopted his or her own way of relating to other members of the congregation. Bob, Carol, Tom, Mae, and Louise at Community Church developed a relationship with the pastor, with each other, and also with the rest of the congregation. Likewise, Sally, Cheryl, Ann, Dolly, Sam, and Charles at Advent Church had a relationship not only with their pastor, but also with each other and with the whole congregation. Leaders have a tendency to model or replicate the leadership style of the pastor. When that pastor leaves, the leaders then become vulnerable to conflict with the members who did not identify with the former pastor's style.

At Community Church each of the people in our story had a connection to the pastor. We, of course, do not have sufficient information about all of these leaders, but we suspect that Carol's and Mae's relationships with the pastor were unusually close. The congregational president, Bob, seemed to have his relationship position in balance. But what about the rest of the congregation? How did each member of the congregation relate to the pastor and to each other?

When the pastor of Community Church announced his retirement, the congregation began to destabilize. Likewise, at Advent Church the congregation's anxiety increased when the pastor resigned, especially since his departure was under pressure. Whenever there is a loss of leadership, the congregational system will lose its balance. (Some systems thinkers call this balance "homeostasis.") This instability creates anxiety within the congregational system. We observe this phenomenon in the world around us.

For example, the United States lost its balance and its stability on the day that President John F. Kennedy was shot. It was important for national stability that the vice president, Lyndon Johnson, was sworn in immediately as president. This is the way the United States Constitution helps the nation lessen its anxiety and return to its natural balance. There was a long period of national grief over Kennedy's death. Some Americans seemed to be more connected to Kennedy than they had realized; his sudden death made that quite apparent. Americans also remember, and so do many other people, that we never related to Lyndon Johnson as we did to Kennedy.

Similarly, at the onset of pastoral transitions, congregations will become de-stabilized. The anxiety level will increase. The congregation will lose sight of its focus, mission, and purpose. Many members will now focus on the loss. If the system was unhealthy at the time of the departure, the anxiety level will increase even further. Soon conflict will develop at a high level. At this time the lay leadership will be especially important in helping the congregation to stabilize.

At Community Church and Advent Church there was, in addition to the loss of the pastor, a significant loss of lay leadership in the congregation. In the midst of this instability, many members may have felt that surely the church was going to sink! As we know from the movie *Titanic*, when we feel we are going to sink, we become reactive quite easily. When members of congregations begin to feel this anxiety deeply, there may be a number of sudden resignations by leaders. This may then contribute to the further destabilizing of the congregation's balance.

The congregation needs to take responsibility for its life and health. After the initial shock of a pastor's resignation, the leaders in a healthy congregation will be able to help steer the congregation onto its right course. It is perhaps at this time, more than at any other time, that the leadership of the congregation becomes aware of their abilities and purposes. It is an opportunity for the congregation to become healthier in its relationships and thus be able to move forward in its life. Leadership changes and shifts in a congregation's power structure are important parts of a pastoral transition. The congregation, as it works together with the intentional interim pastor, will come through these changes stronger and more focused on its mission as a community of faith.

For Reflection and Discussion

1. Reflect upon the last time there was a pastoral transition in your congregation. What leadership changes occurred? What were the significant issues around those changes? Were the issues satisfactorily resolved?

2. What were your personal feelings when your last pastor left the congregation? How did you deal with those feelings? What issues were involved in your feelings? Did you feel like relinquishing your leadership role or even leaving the congregation?

3. What did you learn about your congregation's ability to deal with leadership change?

4. What did you experience in your congregation when the new pastor began his or her ministry?

5. In what ways can the pastoral transition time in your congregation be more positive?

6. What do you see as the role of an interim minister specialist during pastoral transition? Did you have a trained interim pastor during the last transition? Will you have one during the next transition?

CHAPTER 9

Renewing Denominational Linkages

Nancy Miller

It has just been announced. The pastor of Memorial Church is leaving the parish right after Pentecost, some three months away. The whole town is abuzz with the news. But some people, especially the lay leadership of the parish, are beginning to ask, "Now what?"

The answer to that question depends in great measure on a host of variables, the first being the reason for the pastor's departure and the reaction within the parish. Even if the pastor's tenure has been happy, there is some degree of trauma and distress in the departure, because change is not only challenging, but inevitably at least mildly disruptive.

Least traumatic seems to be the departure that is occasioned by the retirement of the pastor, most likely because retirements don't tend to come as big surprises, and especially if the last years of the pastorate were marked by a pre-retirement inertia. One step higher on the stress/trauma scale is the minister leaving one position in order to accept another call. Very often there is some sense of abandonment in the congregation, particularly if people feel that the pastor is leaving too soon. These departures are much less anxious than involuntary separations (when the congregation is unhappy with the pastor), the death or disabling illness of the pastor, or the removal of the pastor for cause (usually for some unethical behavior on the part of the pastor).

Regardless of the circumstances, however, all sorts of opportunities present themselves for the parish whenever a pastor leaves the congregation. One of those opportunities is for the parish and the denomination (judicatory) to engage with each other in new ways. It can indeed be a significant moment, a time when the congregation's relationship to the larger church is lifted up, examined, and refashioned.

Here too are numerous variables, notably the historic relationship between congregation and denomination and the perception of the denomination by the congregation. Is the relationship marked by indifference and passiveness? Is it adversarial in nature? Is it one of cherished partnership? Additionally, relationships are greatly affected by the denominational structures and systems of accountability, especially during an interim between settled pastors. Some denominations, for example, are highly covenantal or voluntary in nature, while others are more systemically hierarchical.

But let's go back to Memorial Church.

It has just been announced. The pastor of Memorial Church is leaving the parish right after Pentecost, some three months away. As it happens, the pastor is retiring.

Imagine the following two possibilities:

Scenario 1. The lay leadership of Memorial Church advises the denominational office immediately. Six weeks later, when no response has been forthcoming, a follow-up call is made, and the denominational representative visits the parish two weeks later.

Scenario 2. The lay leadership of Memorial Church waits until two weeks before the pastor's departure even to advise the denominational office of the situation.

Without doubt, opportunity exists for Memorial Church and the denomination to engage with each other in new ways. It can be a significant moment, a time when the congregation's relationship to the larger church is lifted up, examined, refashioned, and celebrated. Unfortunately, however, the pastor's departure can also bring about friction between congregation and denomination and launch a time when this relationship deteriorates.

No one wants the negative possibilities to occur, nor are they inevitable. But whatever the possibilities, both positive and negative, the time of interim really is a time of opportunity.

The departure of a pastor and the ensuing months of interim time is an opportunity for discernment by the congregation. It is a time to assess their relationship with the denominational authority (by whatever name, be it Bishop, Superintendent, or Judicatory Executive). It is a time to examine the congregation's place within the denomination and in the wider church. It is also a time to ask how those relationships might be strengthened—a time for both congregation and denomination to be present for each other, to provide resources for each other, and to engage the dialogue with positive expectations of each other.

One way to begin that conversation is to review what the relationship has been in the past. Can the congregation recall an instance when the denominational link was not helpful, not available, created difficulties, or caused ill feeling or anxiety? Exactly what happened? How could the outcome have been changed? Did both congregation and denomination express concern or unhappiness in timely and constructive ways? If, for example, as in scenario 1, communications to the denomination remain unanswered, a telephone call before six weeks have gone by might create an atmosphere less charged with annoyance.

Conversely, the parish might recall at least one situation when the denominational connection was constructive, responsive, helpful, and insightful. What specifically happened, and what was positive about it? What did both denomination and congregation do to make it positive?

It is a prime time to ask other questions as well. For example, what does the congregation need from the denomination, not only during the interim time, but in general, and what resources are available? What specific resources are available for the interim time? Does the denominational office offer or provide consultants for the interim process? Does it provide training programs, publicity materials, and the like?

Since relationships are always two-sided coins, there are other pertinent questions. How has the congregation been part of this partnership? What resources does the denomination need and expect from the congregation, and has the congregation made them available? For example, are required reports submitted on a timely basis? Does the congregation participate financially as expected? Do any members of the congregation serve on the councils of the denomination, and is their ministry lifted up and celebrated within the congregation?

Earlier, some rather negative scenarios were presented. Imagine another scenario. The pastor of Memorial Church has just announced that his long-anticipated retirement will take effect immediately after Pentecost, some three months away. The lay leadership of the parish advises the denominational office immediately. The following week, the executive from the denomination communicates with the parish. The essence of the communication is one of pastoral concern and encouragement. Arrangements are made for a Sunday visit in order to celebrate the departing pastor's ministry in that parish and to wish the pastor Godspeed.

The following week Chris, the member of the executive staff who oversees interims, calls to schedule a visit with the governing board some two weeks hence. Chris encourages the board to invite any interested parishioners to attend this meeting.

On the night of the meeting the room is full. The departing pastor is present, as well as several parishioners who are not members of the governing board. The purpose of the meeting is to help the parish anticipate and plan for what lies ahead—the departure of the pastor, as well as the time of self-study and search for a new pastor.

Chris outlines the next steps, speaking not only about what should be addressed before the pastor departs, but also about what will not be especially fruitful activity until after the pastor has gone (see "Do's and Don'ts" at the end of this chapter). For example, although forming a search committee before the pastor leaves would be premature, there is no reason whatever to postpone a good, hard look at parish finances. What is the financial picture? The departing pastor has been full-time; can the parish afford to continue that pattern of ordained leadership?

Chris also takes this opportunity to make sure that the parish conducts an annual review of its books and is fully prepared to suggest names of competent accountants. Chris explains to the group that when it comes time to interview candidates to be their new pastor, the strong and competent candidates will ask whether or not there are annual reviews of the parish accounts.

Chris also challenges the parish leadership, regardless of financial considerations, to ask whether or not the parish needs full-time, ordained leadership? If not, what are the options for the parish to consider, and how would the parish explore those possibilities? Chris talks briefly about such possibilities as forming a partnership with another parish, assembling a cluster of parishes in order to share resources, or perhaps looking for a part-time minister. In the case of Memorial Church, the expectation of continuing with a full-time pastor is grounded in financial reality, and the needs of the parish certainly call for full-time pastoral attention.

Of great concern to most people in the parish is the question of who will lead the parish when the pastor departs. Who will be in the pulpit the Sunday after the pastor leaves? This anxiety is voiced indirectly by a parishioner who wonders why the parish doesn't get on with the search, even before the pastor leaves. Chris is happy to talk about all the reasons why that is not in the best interests of the parish, but the anxiety is relieved only when Chris announces that a trained and experienced interim pastor is available. The board will have an opportunity to meet with that person, and Chris, who has brought along a sample contract for consideration by the parish, offers to assist in negotiating the contract.

Chris speaks at length about the role of an interim minister and outlines some of the ways in which that role is similar to the role of the settled pastor, as well as how the interim minister's role is different. The interim pastor probably won't participate in some activities in the same way as a permanent pastor, but there are other activities that are unique to the interim time which the interim pastor will lead and supervise. In the context of this part of the conversation, Chris outlines briefly the five developmental tasks.

Chris also outlines the function of interim consultants. While interim pastors are clergy who guide parishes in times of transition, interim consultants (lay or clergy) serve as process consultants for the specific work of searching for a new settled pastor. In some denominations, the interim pastor may serve as the consultant; other denominations do not permit both functions to be performed by the same person. Chris has a list of interim consultants, any one of whom can be engaged to lead the parish through the process of discernment, self-study, search, and call. All are competent, trained, and experienced.

The denominational office can provide other resources as well. For example, it will be Chris who conducts a formal exit interview with the departing pastor. Chris also maintains a file of parish profiles that have been assembled by congregations who have recently been in a search process. These profiles can be used as samples as Memorial Church prepares its own profile. The denominational office has demographic information available about the town and surrounding area. It also has a computer program that the calling committee can use to assemble a questionnaire to solicit information from parishioners. There are resources for worship, as the parish celebrates endings and new beginnings. Chris has some suggestions, learned along the way, about choosing a calling committee for the parish.

Chris spends some time reviewing with those present what are normative expectations of the departing pastor. For example, what is denominational wisdom about the former pastor's availability for baptisms, weddings, funerals, or pastoral presence?

And finally, with a particular eye toward strengthening the ties between denomination and congregation, Chris commends one particular section of the Interim Ministry Network's *Basic Education Workbook* called "Toolbox for the Developmental Tasks" by R. Neil Chafin. In an especially strong outline entitled "Rethinking Denominational Linkages," Chafin provides suggestions for encouraging a healthy relationship between congregation and denomination and some concrete signposts for assessing the strengths and the challenges which affect that relationship.

What Chris brings in abundance to this meeting is an ability and willingness to listen, as well as to talk. Chris listens to the questions and takes time not only to answer the questions directly, but also to speak to the concerns that underlie the questions. Chris also leaves a telephone number, a fax number, and an e-mail address with the board, as evidence of a commitment to being available whenever needed.

Throughout the meeting, Chris continues to lift up the overarching purpose that guides all this activity—a lively and vibrant ministry that bears powerful and effective witness to the Good News of Jesus Christ.

The interim time is now launched, and there is optimism on all sides about a positive and productive relationship between the parish and the denomination. That relationship is enhanced both by the work and presence of the consultant, seen properly as an extension of the denominational office's ministry, and by the work of the trained, experienced, and effective interim minister. A sense of teamwork has a chance to develop, instead of a we-they adversarial relationship.

During the interim time the parish engages in an in-depth look at its history, including a review of the historical relationship with the denominational leadership. In the course of that self-examination, the parish notes times of change in the relationship and also notes what the signs have been of good health in that relationship. The parish clearly takes seriously the opportunity for strengthened ties with the denomination, and as evidence of that intention, appoints one member of the calling committee to be in regular touch with Chris as the work of the committee proceeds.

When the calling committee is ready to begin the interview stage of the process, Chris helps the calling committee find qualified and available candidates. Chris also provides helpful insights concerning interview techniques and suggests some questions that have proven to be particularly appropriate for interviewing clergy. At the request of the calling committee, a practice interview is arranged.

When the calling committee has narrowed its search to a few final candidates, the denominational office offers to help check references and to share the cost of any background or credit checks that the parish and denominational policy deem appropriate.

When the interim time comes to a close, Chris also asks the leadership of the parish to participate in the evaluative work. The intention is not to evaluate the new clergy leader, but to help the denomination improve the calling process itself.

In the course of the interim, the parish has felt valued and assisted by the denomination. This is due, in no small measure, to the fact that the denominational personnel served as instruments of wisdom, experience, and assistance, rather than as antagonists committed to red tape and determined to keep the parish jumping through seemingly needless hoops.

For some in the parish, the interim time is the first chance to understand and embrace their denominational identity. For the entire parish it is a time of claiming, in newly articulated ways, what the denominational relationship is and why it is important. It is also a time to articulate why Memorial Church is important to the good health and well-being of the denomination and how its mission and ministry contribute to Christ's great commission to spread the Good News throughout the world.

Do's and Don'ts

For that anxious time after your pastor has resigned, but before your pastor has actually departed.

Do's

1. Pray. Pray, for example, for the parish and for the pastor.
2. Advise the denominational executive.
3. Pray. Pray for the interim time and for the lay leadership of the parish.

4. Invite the denominational representative to a board meeting to talk
5. Pray. Pray for other parishes in transition and for clergy in searches.
6. Celebrate the pastor's ministry.
7. Pray. And trust that God is listening.

Don'ts

1. Don't forget to pray.
2. Don't form a search committee.
3. Don't forget to pray.
4. Don't begin to assemble a parish profile.
5. Don't forget to pray.

For Reflection and Discussion

1. How would you describe your relationship with your denominational office?

2. Can you remember a time when the denomination was a part-ner in mission and ministry with you? What were the circumstances? Who were the players? What, specifically, helped you feel good about the relationship?

3. Who in your congregation is active in the larger denomination? In what capacity?

CHAPTER 10

Commitment to New Directions in Ministry

Philip G. Porcher

It was late summer and the search committee at Faith Church had just informed the board that they were down to four candidates and hoped to have a new pastor by November. Suddenly, however, due to a strange variety of events and circumstances, the search committee found itself with only one candidate. They could have a new pastor as early as September! Panic struck. The board was still pulling together loose ends on the developmental work they had undertaken. The interim pastor had not begun to bring closure to her ministry. And certainly no one was thinking about getting the parsonage or the office ready.

The experience of the search committee at St. Luke's Church was quite different from that at Faith. After a rather long but stimulating interview with the search committee's nominee, St. Luke's Church had excitedly and enthusiastically issued a call to the candidate to become their new pastor. In the discussions and negotiations that followed, the committee discovered that there was a gap of about $10,000 between what the candidate desired (and had rightly assumed would be offered because the search committee knew his present salary) and what the vestry was prepared to offer. After days of serious but anguishing discussion, the two parties just could not reach an agreement. The search committee returned to work, weary but wiser.

Readiness for New Directions

A congregation's approach to that simple word "new" can make a difference in how congregations prepare for ministry with a different pastor. Congregational leaders might be excited and inspired, or they might be filled with caution and guardedness about the implications of an approaching change. Congregations not able to deal with the unexpected or to maintain openness throughout their interim experience will find it difficult to make a commitment to new directions in ministry.

Congregations need to reflect seriously about their readiness for a new direction in ministry. David Odum, Director of the Center for Congregational Health, recently studied two Baptist congregations in North Carolina one year after the completion of an interim period. One of his conclusions points to the chief benefit of a successful interim: Congregations that are truly ready for new directions are better prepared to engage a new pastor.[1] The question for every congregation that has used the interim process and arrived at this stage is: "What have we learned that will help us to engage a new pastor, to begin the relationship with the next pastor on a new basis?"

The last stage in a congregation's transition process, one that happens *after* the interim pastor has left, has been referred to by Loren Mead as "start up."[2] In the first six to twelve months of a new ministry, the congregation and new pastor usually go through a relationship phase commonly referred to as a honeymoon. Then they settle into reality and begin to face the changes and challenges of growing together. This is when the congregation and pastor become truly "engaged."

Congregations that have experienced a successful interim are prepared to engage not only a new pastor, but also a new ministry. Mead indicates that this readiness for new ministry is another benefit of a successful interim. He says, "The installation service is more than the installing of a person into a job, but the installation of a new sense of mission and of an invigorated leadership from laity and a new pastor."[3]

Some congregations minimize the seriousness of the interim period and take a stance that seems to say, "We're ready to get this job over with now!" Other congregations carefully prepare themselves for new relationships and new ministry and thus are able to make a long-term commitment to new directions.

Saying Goodbye to the Interim Pastor

The potential for enthusiasm, creativity, and strong commitment to the
future is clearly present—but waiting to be called forth—in most interim congregations. Sometimes, however, congregations never do quite
get ready for the future. I believe this shortfall is often caused by incomplete closure of the interim. It is easy to neglect this task, especially
if the interim has been a long, hard process and folks are tired. Good
closure generally takes effort on the part of both the interim pastor and
the lay leaders, even under the best of circumstances. The following are
basic aspects of closure to be addressed:

- Wrap up the interim pastor's special tasks and projects. Members
  who participated in these efforts will likely feel discouraged and
  think their time was wasted if tasks are left incomplete.
- Help close out the personal relationships between the interim pastor and members. Help the interim leave as a friend whose ministry
  in this place has ended, but who still cares about the congregation's
  future and who would certainly like to receive your newsletter to
  follow up and keep in touch with your progress!
- Plan a way to celebrate the progress and accomplishments of the
  interim period and to say thanks to all who helped. Create a positive mood to mark the completion of one period before moving on
  to the next.
- In worship, include a liturgy or ritual to say thanks to the search
  committee for their hard work and dedication and to dismiss them
  formally from their charge, symbolizing the end of this part of the
  process.
- Do not avoid the harder aspects of bringing closure to the interim
  period. It is not unusual for misunderstandings and hurt feelings to
  have developed. Some members might feel disappointed about unfinished agendas. The interim pastor and lay leaders will want to
  make every effort to ease such feelings and to seek forgiveness
  where it is called for. One-to-one visits, as well as sensitive liturgical expressions, can be useful when closure is difficult.

Although most of the foregoing aspects of closure would generally
be viewed as routine, others might also need to be considered, depending on circumstances and personalities.

Facing the Future

Excitement and enthusiasm for the future usually increase noticeably when word gets around that the search committee is about to recommend a candidate. That is when the interim pastor and lay board get into high gear. They begin looking at the signs that the congregation is ready for a new pastor. As excitement builds, the interim pastor and leaders need to address the question, "What else do we need to accomplish before the new pastor arrives?"

Most experienced interims know that no matter what they do or say to try to help the congregation slow down and deal carefully with vital issues in the beginning of the interim time, there are always some eager members who begin preparations for the new pastor almost as soon as the former pastor leaves. Some members even begin to get ready for the new pastor before the incumbent has left! Although we sometimes accuse such proactive members of denial or avoidance of important issues, I believe that this behavior is just part of reality for a congregation in transition. It is probably best to accept and work with the attitude rather than fight it.

In general, I like to frame behavior during this time of transition by asking the simple question, "What is the issue here?" This question helps to begin a discussion and avoid unnecessary confrontation. A possible mind-set during the interim time, for instance, might well be fear of the unknown future. Members wonder, "What is going to happen to us now?" Depending on available help and guidance from a consultant, interim pastor, or denominational executive, such a concern can be affirmed and essentially resolved with clear, specific information about what is going to happen in the months ahead.

There are instances, of course, when members might truly be in denial or avoiding issues. Such situations then need to be confronted and resolved. By helping the congregation deal with denial and avoidance throughout the process, the skilled interim pastor helps change the paradigm from one of looking backward to one of facing forward, from dwelling on the past to focusing on the future.

Preparing for a New Beginning

I find that as a congregation moves into this final stage, there are usually several loose ends in the process that still need pulling together before real attention can be given to the new pastor. The first is preparing the lay leadership body for the interview process with the candidate. Careful training can make a significant difference in the outcome of negotiations. No matter what some lay members might say about their own experience with interviewing, the experience for churches is different than that of hiring a new executive for a business!

I believe that an interview by the church board, even after the search committee conducts its own interview before recommending the candidate to the board, is a significant step in the overall process. Such a meeting allows the bonding between board and pastor to begin. It is where the first clues are picked up about how this new relationship is going to work out. It is where the first signs of collaboration or competition will be evident. Even when the entire congregation ultimately decides whether or not to issue the call, it can be very beneficial for the lay governing body to have had a significant period of time and conversation with the candidate before the vote by the congregation. When circumstances prevent such an interview, I would suggest that another formal conversation is valuable even after the congregation's vote, for the reasons mentioned above. Denominational leaders usually have resources for interviewing, including a process guide and examples of questions to be included to make the interview an open dialogue.

A second loose end is the preparation of a letter of agreement, or covenant, between the new pastor and the lay leadership of the congregation. All the work of the self-study that leads to developing goals for the congregation—as well as expectations about the pastor's and lay leaders' roles in completing these goals—should be put in writing. Realizing that not all congregations, and even not all denominations, make use of such a document, I strongly recommend you consider developing one. My long experience with congregations and clergy has convinced me that one of the most frequent sources of misunderstanding and conflict has to do with unclear expectations between pastor and congregation. When the lay leaders work hard to prepare this draft document, they are able to clarify their own expectations of the new pastor. Using this draft in discussion with the candidate will further clarify the relationship. For both parties, about 80 percent of the value of an agreement or covenant is in the dialogue and discussion, and about 20 percent lies in having something written down to review and update as time passes and ministry priorities and expectations change. Further, such a record provides the basis on which to reflect and renegotiate at the first annual review of mutual ministry.

Are We Hiring or Calling?

A third loose end, one of a slightly different nature, tends to be pushed aside late in the interim journey. In the hubbub of activity, time-consuming meetings, and important decision making, many lay leaders just don't seem to get around to the spiritual dimension of the process that is so central to our understanding of the call. Our secular world has much to teach us about systems, skills, methodologies, and techniques. I do not believe, however, that the secular mind knows much about distinguishing between "hiring a new ordained leader" and "calling a new pastor." It is uniquely the church's job to make this distinction. We might be tempted to imitate headhunters searching for a CEO, but I would urge congregational leaders to spend some time discussing and praying about the spiritual dimension of the search process. Is God calling this ordained person and these lay leaders to work together in their mutual ministry in this place and at this time? Sometimes we get the cart before the horse and decide whom we want to hire as our ordained leader and then somehow ask God to bless this action. Surely, as people of faith, we seek God's will and guidance right from the beginning.

Preparing the Way

During this time of preparation for the new future, it is often helpful for the interim pastor or lay leaders to begin to meet with different organizations and groups to talk with them about their hopes, expectations, and concerns regarding the new pastor who will be arriving shortly. Committees and groups appreciate this attention and concern for them, and a meeting focused on the new pastor also helps them understand that there will be yet another shift in the personality and style of ordained leadership. The congregation's newsletter, of course, is a major vehicle through which to communicate with all the members about these issues. Sermons and congregational forums might be used to encourage enthusiasm and support for whatever changes that person will bring. No pastor really does things the same way as another, so members need to be prepared. The new pastor will not be like the former pastor or like the interim pastor, but will be a unique individual whom God and the congregation has called to lead in this community. The hope is that members will be flexible and open enough to welcome another new personality.

Sometimes a congregation will suddenly realize, "The new pastor's coming next month, but we're not ready!" The time of year when a call is issued can have something to do with this phenomenon. If the new pastor will arrive shortly before Advent and Christmas, or Lent and Holy Week, members might wonder how all the planning will get done—or even whether they should begin planning without input from the new pastor. Or folks may have kept hoping all summer that the new pastor would be there to help plan the fall program, and now it is September and nothing has been done. In addition, inadequate communication between the lay board and the search committee or unanticipated events might contribute to a feeling of panic. Or the congregation may still feel divided and disorganized due to poor interim leadership. They are just not ready!

I believe there are two very different categories of questions about readiness that need to be addressed by the interim pastor and the congregation's lay leaders. First, on a corporate level, has the congregation successfully completed the tasks of the interim? Second, on a personal level, have members let go of their feelings and attitudes about the previous pastor? Are they reasonably free from the influence of that pastor? Are they ready to welcome and make a commitment to a new pastor? Readiness on both the corporate and personal levels is essential before the congregation can move on.

Getting Ready to Say Hello

In addition to addressing these organizational issues, there are many practical things a congregation can do to prepare to welcome the new pastor and to demonstrate that the old has passed away and the new is coming.

- Some interim pastors like to leave a care packet for the new minister with pastoral information about certain members who need prompt attention, people who may be ill or have special needs. Notes about upcoming events which have already been planned or which require immediate planning or preparation are helpful. Information about parish or family crises might be appreciated. Some new pastors are appreciative and like to receive such information. Some, however, prefer to discover that kind of information on their own and hope to avoid any bias or prejudice that might creep in, however unintentionally, through another's messages.
- Some congregations will need to address the condition of the pastor's study and decide what, if anything, needs to be done before the new pastor arrives. Maybe it needs repainting, a clean or new carpet, or general freshening up. It is usually best if lay leaders check with the new pastor to find out what he or she prefers, determine what the congregation can afford, and get the work done before the pastor's arrival. Certainly the interim pastor's books and other belongings should be out of the study well before the new pastor arrives. This action has an interesting and helpful psychological side effect as members observe an empty office for a few weeks. They seem to appreciate it more when it is filled again!
- Some denominational leaders recommend that congregations use "supply clergy" for a few weeks between the last Sunday of the interim and the new pastor's first Sunday. This practice gives the congregation an emotional breather to get ready for the next phase. It also emphasizes that the interim leader is indeed gone and enhances anticipation for the new leader. Not all denominations and circumstances support this approach, however.
- At the first worship service conducted by the new pastor, neither the interim pastor nor an interim consultant should be present. This is widely accepted ministerial protocol. The day belongs solely to the new pastor and the congregation. At a later date, however, usually in conjunction with a service of recognition or installation, the interim leaders might be invited back to share the congregation's joy in the new ministry. These leaders would sit with the congregation as friends, however, rather than participating in leading the worship service. There are, of course, denominational differences in how these matters are to be handled.

- The lay leaders might establish a support group to help the new pastor and family get settled and oriented in their new surroundings. Such a transition team is a way lay leaders can be reminded of and practice their need to care for their pastor, right from the beginning. This approach might be especially helpful in large congregations with many groups and individuals to meet.

Evaluating the Interim Time

The use of evaluations of any kind at the close of the interim period seems to be decreasing rather than increasing. Perhaps this decrease is because most clergy and congregations have not had good experiences with evaluations. That is why I prefer the model of mutual ministry review. Evaluation tends to be one-sided, and mutual review is a way to reflect on common ministry and relationships.

Intentionality on the part of the lay leadership is important if any worthwhile mutual ministry review is to happen. But I have long believed it is in the self-interest of each interim pastor to ask what he or she might have done better, or at least differently. Lay leaders can also learn from an evaluation by discovering what has been useful and constructive about the process, as well as by noting what congregational issues might still be unresolved. Even though they may not like to think about a future interim time, an evaluation of the current one might help a congregation use an interim more effectively next time. And there will be a "next time" eventually!

Does All This Work Matter?

Indeed it does! As much as possible needs to be done during the interim time to help the congregation become more unified; to increase understanding and commitment for its work; to develop as clear a vision, mission, and identity as possible; and to get off to the best possible beginning with the new pastor. The beginning of a new ministry is very important in relation to the years that are to follow. High resolve is required, however, if the interim pastor and congregation are to work together effectively, find the right person to be the congregation's next ordained leader, say good-bye to the old, and welcome the new. What inspires and strengthens us for this task is the knowledge that as the people of God, we all seek to find and do the ministry to which God is calling us. That calling deserves our prayers, our commitment to work together, and our intention to complete the interim process with the same enthusiasm and integrity with which we began.

For Reflection and Discussion

1. After reading this chapter, what issues or insights strike you as most significant for your congregation?

2. What might be done about these issues?

3. Which closure issues for the interim period seem most problematic for your congregation?

4. Given all of your work and reflection during this interim, how will your congregation's relationship with your new pastor be different?

5. How do your congregation's leaders distinguish between calling and hiring?

6. What needs to be done in your congregation before you are ready for your new pastor?

7. What are the signs in your congregation that you are ready to move into a new future and to receive a new leader?

PART 3

Framing the Journey

CHAPTER 11

The Biblical and Theological Basis for Interim Ministry

Warren Schulz

"Do not be conformed to this world but be transformed by the renewing of your minds, so that you may discern what is the will of God, what is good and acceptable and perfect" (Rom.12:2).

This chapter uses three words: *change*, *transition*, and *transformation*. Although these three concepts are connected, they are not synonymous. For clarity, I prefer to define them as follows:

Change: The inevitable movement of life's forces.
Transition: The process by which we must deal with the inevitable changes of life (the interim).
Transformation: The new shape that occurs after transition, toward which change is aimed.

Now let us move directly to the heart of our Christian faith. God acts to *change* the horrible consequence of sin into forgiveness. The process of *transition* occurs as Jesus pours out his blood from a cross on Golgotha. Easter morn and a joyous resurrection present a *transformation* to new life with new shape.

In theology, this whole movement of change, transition, and transformation through a cross and resurrection is the Good News that is our mission to proclaim. The Greek word for this good news story of cross to resurrection is *evangel*, from which we derive the English word *evangelism*. Congregations are not only the proclaimers of change, transition, and transformation through their evangelism; they are also living examples of it.

Although the church is often described as being resistant to change, its basic rituals celebrate it! The presence of God in Christ is invoked and celebrated during the four major transitions of an individual's life. Rituals celebrate them. Birth (baptism), puberty (confirmation), marriage (wedding), and death (funeral) summon to the church even the most inactive of a congregation's members. For Christians the journey of life encompasses a changing dynamic with at least these four transition rituals, which express letting go of what was and moving ahead into a transformed future. The church, it could be said, is an expert in transition!

Although the church is often described as being resistant to change, much of its effort centers on proclaiming the gospel in an ever-changing world. The task of determining God's will is a constant theological struggle. The church *should* be an expert in transition!

Although the church is often described as being resistant to change, the church nevertheless rests its case on the biblical witness that tells a moving, changing story of God's actions throughout history. The witness of Scripture describes major transitions in God's relationship to the world. God created the world, established a covenant through Abraham, delivered Israel from Egypt through Moses, and won for us eternal salvation through Jesus Christ. The church is called out to proclaim faithfully the story of God's people in transition.

Having then these theological understandings rooted deeply within our belief systems, one would assume the church to be an expert in the process of transition. As God's people, we are especially tuned in to a God described as more "verb" than "noun." We relate to God who moves, does things, gives vision of the future (just as God would empower us to do), rather than a God presented as a stationary idol. Gathered by God, Christ's church is the vehicle to move us, again and again, toward new transformations.

Why then do transition times so often not receive enthusiastic applause within the church? We certainly have noticed that transition gets little applause anywhere, because transition means struggle. It is often a wilderness experience. At its best, transition causes anxiety; at its worst, it causes pain. We want to avoid as much pain and struggle as possible. Yet, in divine wisdom, God consistently allows us to experience it. It is as if God has created us so that we grow through change and the transition that accompanies it. Over and over again we are thrust by change into dying to something, sinking into a chaos or despair, and then rising again to something new. Think how many times you have made this loop in minor and major ways. The more we experience this journey, the more it seems we are struck by the central message of our Christian faith: Resurrection is won through the cross, and there is a time of transition between Good Friday and Easter Sunday.

"On the third day he rose again!" The formulators of the two great Christian creeds (Apostles' and Nicene) made sure they included this phrase. The early church leaders were certain of an interim period of three days between the death and resurrection of Jesus! After all, what a transition! This Jesus, as the writers of the creeds articulated, lived in the Roman world of the first century (born of the Virgin Mary, suffered under Pontius Pilate), and expanded his realm into the eternal heavens where he would "sit on the right hand of God." Although today we would rightly argue that Christ was present even at the creation, we can appreciate what a leap of faith these early disciples had to make from seeing Jesus walking the dusty roads of Palestine as their rabbi and a healing miracle worker; to seeing their Master crucified, dead, and buried; and finally, to seeing a risen Christ, a Christ of the cosmos! What a transformation!

Although change is occurring all the time in life and constantly forcing us into transition modes, there are major pivotal points in our individual lives (and certainly in our corporate life as a congregation) where we must listen for the Holy Spirit to guide us.

Scripture is rich with examples of special transition times (interim times) that God's people experienced. These were pivot times, times of renewal, times to make a turn. These were times when God chose special leaders to guide the people in the struggle toward transformation. These leaders helped the people deal with the grief of letting go of the past. They walked the wilderness with them and reminded them of the promise of the new. When the people arrived at the threshold of the new, the leadership mantle was passed on to someone who would lead during the transformation period, usually a time that was more stable and would endure, at least until the next major change.

At least two stories from Scripture offer helpful examples of periods in the journey of God's people that were preludes to major transformation. These preludes were interim times, times of transition. The biblical writers were clear that God's hand was directing these events as part of God's redemptive mission. And today God continues to lead the church through transition to transformation, through death to resurrection.

God purposely created a buffer zone—an interim time or interval needed for the tremendous transition of moving those humbled, bewildered disciples from the cross (the end) to the new beginning (the resurrection). It was St. Luke who gave us a most wonderful story of Jesus donning the role of an interim pastor, as it were, and working the five developmental tasks no less! Read the story in Luke 24:13-35 and 48-53 and think about the transition going on in the minds of the disciples. We can easily translate this marvelous story into interim ministry terms.

As any trained interim pastor would do, Jesus made a quick entry into the midst of these despairing disciples and invited them to discuss the pain they felt. Jesus skillfully made himself part of the group yet remained outside of it, which allowed him to help with their grief work so they could talk about it and avoid denial.

In despair this little congregation of disciples wandered aimlessly in what today we would call dysfunction. Maybe that is why some decided to take the walk to Emmaus. They were expressing hopelessness. Beneath their quandary could be heard comments like: "Now what do we do? Our leader has left!" Jesus moves quickly to the interim task of helping the disciples *come to terms with their history* (the first developmental task). They had forgotten that part of their past had to be retold in order to give them hope for their future:

> Then he said to them, "Oh, how foolish you are, and how slow of heart to believe all that the prophets have declared! Was it not necessary that the Messiah should suffer these things and then enter into his glory?" Then beginning with Moses and all the prophets, he interpreted to them the things about himself in all the scriptures (Luke 24:25-27).

Sharing the disciples' loneliness, Jesus consents to spending time with them at a meal. Breaking bread together becomes a healing and revealing act as Jesus leads them into *discovering a new identity* (the second developmental task):

> When he was at the table with them, he took bread, blessed and broke it, and gave it to them. Then their eyes were opened, and they recognized him; and he vanished from their sight (Luke 24: 30-31).

The disciples' discovery of the new reality of Christ's continual presence is the beginning of a great future:

They said to each other, "Were not our hearts burning within us while he was talking to us on the road, while he was opening the scriptures to us?" (Luke 24:32)

The two disciples cannot contain their enthusiasm. The hope that is in Christ must be shared:

That same hour they got up and returned to Jerusalem; and they found the eleven and their companions gathered together. They were saying: "The Lord has risen indeed, and he has appeared to Simon!" Then they told what had happened on the road, and how he had been made known to them in the breaking of the bread (Luke 24:33-35).

It is as though Jesus, the interim pastor, was furthering the task we call *renewing linkages* (the third developmental task), a process that began with a meal and inspired them to hurry back to Jerusalem where the larger church was meeting.

Jesus, in his short role as interim pastor, has now also managed some *leadership shifts* (the fourth developmental task). No longer would the rabbi from Nazareth be there to instruct and lead his followers. He would be leaving this to new leadership from among these newly equipped disciples:

You are witnesses of these things. And see, I am sending upon you what my Father has promised; so stay here in the city until you have been clothed with power from on high (Luke 24:48-49).

The final developmental task was about to be engaged. It was now the time *to commit to a new future* (the fifth developmental task).

Then he led them out as far as Bethany, and, lifting up his hands, He blessed them. While He was blessing them, He withdrew from them and was carried up into heaven. And they worshipped him, and returned to Jerusalem with great joy; and they were continually in the temple blessing God (Luke 24:50-53).

The *change* was the plan of God. The *transition* was guided by Jesus in a way similar to interim pastoral care. *Transformation* into the new beginning would begin soon on Pentecost Day when there would be unveiled the "new" body of Christ—the church!

God must like transition spaces (wilderness experiences) because God sure creates a lot of them. A major part of the Old Testament deals with the Exodus event. It is a document of a transition or interim time during which God's people roam the wilderness under the leadership of their "interim pastor," Moses. The same dynamics of transition occur among the people as occur in many of our congregations during an interim today.

Change is orchestrated by God. It is inevitable. The Israelites were under bondage in Egypt. They were held as slaves and thus had become impotent to do the mission to which God had called them. The covenant with Abraham had been that this nation of Israel was to be a blessing to the world. They were to be God's proclaimers. The covenant from God had also promised that they would have a land of their own and become a nation. The Israelites themselves prayed for a change in their situation. They were ready for a move from bondage to freedom, from being enslaved tenants in a foreign place to a land they would call their own. Like so many congregations, they at first eagerly welcomed change, but it soon became apparent that they were not at all prepared for the struggle that transition brings. Up until the time of the departure from Egypt, Moses had pretty well set the stage. He had done the work of contracting with the people and negotiating with the pharaoh. Moses, as a good interim pastor, contracted well and gave the assurance of future hope to the people. Again and again Moses reminded the Hebrew people of God's presence as they entered the wilderness of transition.

> The Lord went in front of them in a pillar of cloud by day, to lead them along the way, and in a pillar of fire by night, to give them light, so that they may travel by day and by night. Neither the pillar of cloud by day nor the pillar of fire by night left its place in front of the people (Exod. 13:21-22).

But the process of transition does cause some fearful moments along the way, even with divine presence and a strong interim pastor! Pharaoh changed his mind and angrily pursued the Israelites after they had marched hopefully out of Egypt toward the promised land. How logical their fear was; the Egyptian soldiers were coming at them from behind, and in front of them was the Red Sea. They became psychologically and physically frozen, unable to go forward or backward. In interim ministry we define such situations as critical moments. Something has to give.

> But Moses said to the people, "Do not be afraid, stand firm, and see the deliverance that the Lord will accomplish for you today; for the Egyptians whom you see today you shall never see again. The Lord will fight for you, and you have only to keep still (Exod. 14:13-14).

One would think that experiencing the saving hand of God would establish such a profound faith that the Israelites would continue their transition journey singing, "On Our Way Rejoicing"! After all, God through Moses saved them from Pharaoh's army. Moses lifted high his staff, parted the Red Sea, and the people moved on. How could they forget this? They do. So do we. Maybe this is one answer to the question, "Why does God, over and over again, fill our lives with so many transition times?" Maybe, just maybe, it is because, as humans, we are slow learners. We have to hear and experience the story over and over again. We must stay in touch with our history. It isn't very long into the journey of transition wilderness when God's people again become anxious.

> The whole congregation of the Israelites complain against Moses and Aaron in the wilderness. The Israelites said to them, "If only we had died by the hand of the Lord in the land of Egypt, when we sat by the fleshpots and ate our fill of bread; for you have brought us out into this wilderness to kill this whole assembly with hunger." Then the Lord said to Moses, "I am going to rain bread from heaven for you, and each day the people shall go out and gather enough for that day" (Exod. 16:2-4).

The Israelites were faced with another change. The transformation to which they were headed was that of an independent nation. They knew what it was like to be in slavery where everything was dictated and organized for them. Now they would have to see themselves as a new and different community. In interim ministry language, the system was changing. As a congregation experiences growth and moves toward a new identity as an organization, there is often longing for the time when they were held together by a "family" feel. Sometimes a congregation discovers that it must move from being an organism to an organization. The interim time becomes the time when new blueprints for ministry are drawn. Moving from the "old" to the "new" is seldom without stress and conflict. As with the ancient Israelites, whose transition was a major one, congregations in transition often experience the same feelings today.

Moses discovered he needed the aid of a consultant, Jethro. Today, congregations in an interim period may also need an outside consultant. Jethro also happens to be Moses' father-in-law who came to visit him in the wilderness one day. Helpful is the fact that Jethro himself is a priest. Being an outsider, it is very easy for Jethro to be more observant and objective than just about anyone else in the camp. He watches Moses trying to be everything to everybody. Moses is operating as if he were the pastor of a small, family-sized congregation. Like many in our congregations today, the Israelites no doubt also liked their pastor to be available for them at any hour. Moses had very little time for self-care or for his own family. Jethro had come to bring his daughter back to her husband, Moses. She had been living at home with Dad; she belonged with her husband. It was perhaps providential that Jethro came when he did.

Jethro observed Moses in action. He found Moses working from morning until evening with lines of people coming to him for spiritual advice as well as counseling. Jethro emphatically asks Moses:

> Why are you trying to do this alone? What you are doing is not good. You will surely wear yourself out, both you and these people. Now listen to me and I will give you counsel (Exod. 18:17-19).

This good advice was heeded and a new structure emerged, better suited for the future mission of God's people.

When is the interim period accomplished? Often we think we can easily plot this on a timeline. An interim can be too short or too long. It seemed like the time was ripe for the Israelites to enter their promised land. Forty years had now gone by and they finally stood at the border of their new land. Eventually, the end of the transition had arrived. It was now time for the transformation to begin. Moses was like an interim pastor. He specialized in transition, not transformation. His interim call was completed.

Just as a modern church calls a new pastor, it was time for the new leadership in Israel. Joshua would become the transformational leader. Sometimes the distinction between an interim pastor and a regularly called pastor is that the transformational pastor is referred to as a "settled" pastor. Joshua would now set about to putting some substance to the plans and dreams blueprinted during the transition.

God must certainly like transition, for it is pumped into the very heart of the creation. *Change, transition, and transformation* parallel with *death, three days, and resurrection.* They also parallel with *exodus from Egypt, the wilderness, and entrance into Canaan.* They become the living history of every congregation.

For Reflection and Discussion

1. To what extent do you think your congregation resists change? Celebrates it? Give examples of each response.

2. When have you experienced the Holy Spirit speaking to you through a time of transition? How did things change for you as a result?

3. Think of a person in the Bible who experienced great change. How did this person respond to the change? What was difficult about the experience? What was positive?

4. In this chapter I wrote, "Change is orchestrated by God." Do you agree or disagree? Why?

5. What could your congregation learn about change and the interim from the story of the exodus?

CHAPTER 12

Ethical Dimensions of the Interim Time

Thomas A. Hughart

Tom Williams, interim pastor at St. Matthew's Church, was a bit surprised when a parishioner remarked at coffee hour one Sunday, "I guess being an interim minister is easier than having a permanent parish. The denomination has less control over what you do and there's a lot less pressure. Right?"

Tom's response was a considered one.

"Well, in some ways interims have a harder job," he replied. "We have all the regular tasks of pastoral ministry, plus we are called to help manage change. And we are as responsible for our behavior and performance as any installed pastor is."

The ethical issues involved in interim ministry need to be seen within the context of professional ethics for all ministry. Interim ministers, like all others, maintain an ethical stance in order to advance the cause of Jesus Christ, to strengthen and build up the body of Christ, and to equip the congregation for mission in the church and the larger community. All ministers, as God's servants, follow the Lord Jesus Christ, love their neighbors, and work for the reconciliation of the world. They work for the peace, unity, and purity of the Church, and they serve society with honest intelligence, integrity, and love.

The Contracting Process: A Good Beginning

Ethical issues are raised throughout the interim period for both church and minister. Beginning with the negotiation of a contract, the dynamic of the transitional ministry is established. Honest negotiation involves recognition of the interim pastor's value as a professional, as well as the pastor's financial and time commitments and a mutual appreciation of the financial structure of the congregation being served. Intentional interim ministers do not limit themselves to financially well-off congregations, but are willing to serve wherever their skills and abilities fit a congregation's needs. Congregations do not view the interim time as a chance to save money. Rather, it is in the long-term best interest of congregations to maintain budgeted levels of ministerial support. In most cases the terms of call of the previous pastor set the terms of call for the interim. At the very least, recommended compensation minimums set by denominations should always be honored by congregations.

After the contract has been established and ratified by higher authorities, as required by the congregation's denominational policy, it should be honored and reviewed periodically, at least every six months. Circumstances may have changed, particularly for interims who are commuting or who have relocated a considerable distance. The time for renewal of a contract is also an opportunity for re-negotiation and should be an occasion for recommitment to the goals and tasks of interim ministry.

The contracting process is the beginning of an ethical covenant between the congregation and the pastor, a process that sets the framework of the interim journey, clarifies boundaries, and focuses expectations for the time of transition. The beginning of an interim ministry is not only about finances and a contract; it is also about recognizing a new relationship between a congregation and the pastor who comes to serve during the time of transition. Soon after the interim pastor's starting Sunday, if not actually on that day, a service of recognition and welcome should take place to celebrate the new relationship and to lift up the challenge of the interim period.

The Question of Candidacy

A major and crucial issue must be clearly understood from the outset of an interim relationship between pastor and people: *The interim pastor shall not be a candidate for the installed position.* All denominations consider this a cardinal principle of interim ministry. The interim's candidacy is an ethical issue for both congregation and interim pastor.

The congregation is constrained from suggesting it, and the interim pastor from considering it. This policy should be stated in the interim pastor's contract and communicated clearly to the congregation through a letter, newsletter articles, and other means.

The rationale for this universal policy is rooted in concern for the long-term health of congregations. The issue is one of maintaining a fair and level playing field for all candidates, recognizing that anyone who has provided any kind of ministry in a congregation has a tendency to develop loyalties and thus should be disqualified as a candidate. During the interim time the congregation is uniquely anxious and vulnerable and may do itself a disservice by choosing the interim without giving due consideration to a wider field of candidates. The higher visibility of the interim minister also gives the interim an advantage over other potential candidates. Further, experience has shown that when an interim becomes a candidate, there is an increased potential for conflict in the congregation down the road as hidden resentments about the curtailed search process surface. The congregation and interim pastor must make a solemn commitment not to abrogate the non-candidacy rule.

Respecting Different Gifts

Every interim pastor follows a series of predecessors. Congregations need to be aware that ministerial ethics prohibit pastors from making value judgments about colleagues who have preceded them. We need to remember Paul's wise advice to the ancient Corinthian church: "I planted, Apollos watered, but God gave the growth" (1Cor. 3:6, RSV). All positive contributions to ministry should be honored. It is not helpful for church members to make comparisons between the interim and his or her predecessor, or to seek comments about that leader from the interim. Nothing constructive is to be gained by such conversation. The focus needs to be on the present and future, not the past.

This is not to say, however, that people should be inhibited from expressing honest feelings related to the departure of a beloved pastor or, if there has been misconduct, openly sharing pain and disappointment. Many interim congregations do need to complete closure about the previous pastorate, a process that is helped by the sharing of feelings, but this needs to be accomplished as much as possible in a nonjudgmental way.

One of the functions of the interim pastor is to model a different
style of ministry as a way of sensitizing the congregation to the fact that
the next permanent pastor will certainly be a different person and a
leader with unique gifts. The ethics of the interim journey call us to con-
centrate on the question of what leadership needs and skills are essential
to the church in order that God's mission may be furthered. To dwell on
personalities, or on past failures and mistakes, will not move the congregation forward in positive ways.

Sharing Leadership Faithfully

Congregations should not consider the interim pastor as being "in
charge" of the church. Intentional interim ministers understand their
role as that of coach or guide to the elected leadership of the parish.
The interim pastor's challenge is to guide a process of transition, not
assume the reins of leadership from the laity. Lay leaders have an ethical mandate to serve the church conscientiously for their terms of office.
Churches that benefit most from interim ministry are those in which the
congregational leadership takes active responsibility for the developmental tasks, while allowing the interim pastor to guide and support the
overall process.

The Interim Pastor's Relationship to the Search

A central aspect of the interim journey is the search for a new permanent
pastor. It is important that the congregation understand the relationship
of the interim leader to that crucial task. The intentional interim pastor
recognizes the risks involved in trying to define the role of the next pastor. It is not the interim pastor's province. He or she should not be asked
by the nominating committee or search committee for advice pertaining
to the search. Such advice properly comes from the denominational office. Names of candidates should not be divulged to the interim pastor.
Interim pastors have been trained to insulate themselves from the search
process. It is not appropriate for a search or call committee to ask associate pastors or interim pastors to inform them about theological biases,
role models, or even job descriptions that will fit their particular understanding of ministry. The interim pastor might supply members of the

committee with mission statements, annual reports, and books and periodicals that can help them discover new visions of ministry, but it is not ethical for the interim pastor to try to shape or describe the role of the person being sought.

Sometimes members of the committee may seek out the interim pastor for information about candidates, or the candidates may seek out the interim for information about the congregation. In such situations it is extremely important for members of the committee to seek out objective sources of information, rather than expecting the interim to share personal reflections, prejudices, or previous experiences. Search committee members should be aware that after a candidate has been chosen, it is then appropriate for the interim minister to share copies of any reports that have been filed with denominational bodies about the experience of interim ministry in that place. It may also be appropriate for the interim pastor to share observations about the theological stance of the congregation, the nature of the community, and the advantages and disadvantages of the particular situation as it has been experienced, but not in a way that would prejudice the candidate's own personal evaluation of the opportunity being presented.

Boundary Issues in the Interim Time

Possibly the most difficult ethical issues during the interim time have to do with boundaries. Congregations need to deepen their understanding of such dynamics. Both interim pastors and congregational leaders need to understand what type of relationship is appropriate between congregants and the previous pastor. Certainly what constitutes a life-giving relationship depends in part on the circumstances under which the previous pastor left the congregation. Former pastors who were involved in sexual misconduct, for example, are clearly banned by ecclesiastical authorities from continuing ministry, nor would congregations want them to do so.

Beloved pastors from former years who continue to maintain relationships or provide pastoral service to former congregants pose a different problem. When relationships with former pastors are being used as a way of undermining the development of new pastoral relationships or as a way of showing passive-aggressive behavior toward the interim pastor, then such relationships need to be confronted. To be pastoral, however, it may be necessary to invite a former pastor to share in officiating at a wedding or funeral. But it should always be clear that the interim or the new pastor is in charge and presiding. It is preferable to encourage the previous pastor to show concern and pastoral care by phoning, sending cards or notes, or by attending like any other guest. The previous pastor's participation may imply that there is something missing in the way the interim is conducting the service.

Previous pastors who continue to receive perquisites or to perform pastoral functions for former parishioners interfere with the opportunities for establishing new pastoral relationships. In extreme cases it may be necessary for denominational officials to exercise some restraint on the activities of previous pastors, even to the extent of denying them permission to "labor inside the bounds" of their old parish or district, or to "labor outside the bounds" of the governing body in which they now reside.

Staff Relationships

Frequently, an underlying cause for the departure of the previous pastor is difficult staff relationships. It may, therefore, fall to the lot of the interim pastor to be the one who encourages incumbent staff members to move on before a new pastor arrives. If needed staff changes are not made, the new pastor may find it necessary, soon after beginning the pastorate, to make staff changes and thus subject himself or herself to all the criticism that goes with such changes. This is surely not a good way to begin a new pastorate.

In some denominations it is standard policy that when a pastor resigns, remaining staff are advised that their resignations should be on the desk of the newly selected pastor when that person arrives. In other denominations those resignations are post-dated some months so that the new pastor has the option of keeping those persons, or accepting their resignations. When staff positions need to be filled, it is important that incumbent staff be informed as to whether or not they will be considered for the position.

Ordinarily, certain program people who are not directly connected to the pastoral care functions of the church, such as nursery school directors, building managers, or choir directors, may be retained through several pastorates. However, in multiple staff situations where strong advocates are seeking to promote the candidacy of an associate or assistant pastor for the senior position—often in competition with the search committee—it then becomes important that staff changes be made during the interim. One reason for this is to forestall conflict in the congregation. An equally important reason is to take the onus for such change away from the incoming senior pastor. Intentional interim pastors understand their role in these situations and are ready to accept the sometimes stressful reactions from congregants.

Other Ethical Areas

Many of the boundary issues for interim pastors are the same as those for any other pastor. These boundaries require that ministers limit their practice to those positions and responsibilities for which they are qualified; that during counseling they maintain the relationship on a professional basis; that they know how to make referrals if that is indicated either by the complexity of the situation or by the transference that is being experienced by either party; and that they keep notes and records secure and all communications confidential. It is also the duty of a minister not to make unrealistic promises about the outcome of professional services, nor to take any unfair advantage either of a person or a position, and to avoid disparagement of any person, especially colleagues and other professionals. And, of course, ministers do not engage in sexual misconduct with their clients or any other members of the congregations they serve.

Ministers also need to recognize the powerful emotional influence they have and therefore use care and sensitivity in dealing with all people. While holding strongly to their own theological convictions, they must at the same time be careful not to force their beliefs upon others, respecting the integrity and freedom of each person to find his or her own faith.

The Ethics of Exiting: Ending the Interim

Determining the time for the departure of an interim can also be an ethical issue for both the congregation and the interim pastor. For the interim pastor, "jumping ship" prematurely in order to take advantage of another opportunity, particularly if it is more attractive than the present one, raises ethical issues. However, if it is determined that the church is really not committed to the purposes of interim ministry, or that lay leadership is finding that the present interim is not effectively helping the congregation through its tasks, then it may be wise for the interim to resign or for the congregation to ask for that resignation. It is generally understood that an interim minister will bring the congregation to the point where it is ready to commit itself to a new visionary mission statement and to give its loyalty to a new pastor.

Agreement also needs to be reached regarding the actual date of leaving. Contract extensions that are made because the interim pastor wants to extend the opportunity or is enjoying the benefits more than the duties are not ethical. When the congregation has selected its next pastor and worked out the date for beginning, then the contract with the interim pastor should be negotiated toward a closing. Optimally, the interim pastor will leave on one day and the new pastor will arrive on the next. For the new pastor some overlap might be beneficial for such purposes as meeting staff, being introduced to officers of the church, and getting settled in the community. However, no agreements should be made for the provision of pastoral ministry by the interim after the arrival date of the new pastor. Any previous commitments should be honored only with the permission of the new pastor, and these commitments should be made known at the beginning of the new pastor's tenure.

The congregation needs to be given an opportunity to bid farewell and to express appreciation to the interim pastor. It may be possible for the interim pastor to retain some friendships with parishioners in the congregation, but these should never include discussion of church programs, policies, or relationships.

During the interim journey, as the congregation and its intentional interim pastor work together with integrity, the ultimate goal is to bring a congregation to the point of knowing and accepting where it has been, of being able to define where it is and where it wants to go, and of having the ability to commit itself to a new vision and new leadership as it moves into the future.

For Reflection and Discussion

1. As your church moves into the interim period, how do you see the people responding to the interim leader? Are there hints about getting him or her to stay?

2. What do you see as some of the issues regarding ministerial ethics in your congregation in the past?

3. What is your congregation's relationship now to its previous pastors? Has closure been accomplished?

4. Discuss this statement: The congregation and pastor share equally the responsibility for ethical relationships.

5. How do you think the congregation should handle breaches in ethics?

PART 4

Tools for the Journey

TOOL 1

The Transitional Steering Team

Robert W. Johnson

My career as an Interim Ministry Specialist in many congregations of the United Church of Canada has led me to value a partnership with congregational leaders that I have called the transitional steering team. During the interim period in churches I have served, it has been immensely helpful to organize a special leadership group to guide an intervention into the life of the congregation for the purpose of renewal and transformation. The transitional steering team works closely with the interim pastor to plan and guide a process that will bring about needed change and prepare the congregation for a new future. The purpose of the transitional steering team is:

- To help congregational members heal after the loss of their pastor and to gain perspective on the chapter in their lives that has ended
- To gather the feelings and ideas of both members and non-members of the congregation about their church in a time of change
- To provide a forum for the sharing and focusing of hopes and aspirations for the future
- To help the congregation move from preoccupation with the past to a state of readiness for a new chapter in its life under the leadership of a new pastor
- To involve the congregation in accomplishing the developmental tasks of the interim period.

The members of the transitional steering team are committed to the unique opportunity presented in the interim time. It is a time of high challenge for the congregation, a time for self-assessment, and a time for visioning and recommitment to mission and ministry.

The congregation is helped to gain perspective on its past and to focus on its future. The overall goal is to bring the congregation to a condition of health, unity, and readiness to move forward under the leadership of a new pastor.

Effective lines of communication between the transitional steering team and the congregation are crucial. The interim pastor will take care to see that such communication takes place on a regular basis. He or she may designate a person to be the liaison between the team and the church board. In addition, full support of the broader church leadership is essential to make the most of the interim opportunity. The widest possible ownership of ideas and decisions regarding the congregation's future is to be sought.

A transitional steering team may be formed in different ways, depending upon the operating procedures in place in a particular congregation. Usually, four to six active members of the congregation will be needed to serve in this capacity during the interim period. Insofar as possible, the members of the team should represent a cross section of the congregation's membership. It is important that the people selected for the transitional steering team have a vision of what can happen during the interim journey of the congregation, because the congregation is in what might be called "open space"—a time between what was and what will come—and the team is responsible for charting a course that will move the people of the faith community into the future. An official recognition of the team by the congregation, possibly by a liturgical action during Sunday worship, would be helpful in formalizing its role as a significant group during the interim period.

In his book *Dry Bones Breathe* Robert Worley writes: "Members activate themselves. Leaders cannot activate others. They can model behaviors appropriate for church members to lead charismatically."[1] This statement suggests to me that transitional steering team members will need to practice what I call "appropriate behavior" during this critical phase of the beginning of the transformation process. They must value each member's contributions and take suggestions and ideas seriously. They must be willing to listen. They must be willing to become acquainted with resources for gathering and evaluating information. They must honor confidentiality. The trust of the church membership is essential for the team members if they are to be successful in leading a process of change.

The transitional steering team will need to become familiar with resources made available by the interim minister for the purpose of gathering the information needed to create a congregational vision, establish goals, and define activities for the future ministry of the church. A major task for the team will be the collation and interpretation of information gathered from the congregation about its life and vision of the future. This information will become a crucial guide for the search committee in their eventual interviews with potential candidates for the new pastorate. In cooperation with the interim minister, the transitional steering team will take responsibility for bringing closure to the information-gathering process. Sometimes this is done in the context of a worship service during which appreciation is expressed for everyone's contributions that have resulted in an accurate profile of the congregation and an exciting vision of its future. Following the service, a special fellowship hour could celebrate what has been accomplished. Subsequently, the transitional steering team may take responsibility for monitoring the progress of the congregation toward the objectives and activities it has mapped out for itself as it begins a new chapter in its life under the leadership of a newly called pastor.

Our Christian faith places the resurrection of Jesus Christ at the center of the church's life, reminding us that God's power is always at work in transforming the church God has called into being. The apostle Paul reminds us that in Christ all things are made new (2 Cor. 5:17). Responding to God's love in Word and Sacrament, the transitional steering team helps generate a spirit of hope and anticipation as the congregation moves into new directions of mission and ministry in the name of Jesus Christ.

Bible Studies for the Journey

Janet Parsons Mackey and Barbara W. Miner

The Purpose of the Bible Study

The purpose of the Bible study is to offer a simple and straightforward way to name and understand the interim experience, a time that can be confusing and complex in the life of a congregation. The series is designed to address the five developmental tasks of the interim period, yet the experiential nature of the design can provide an opportunity to get in touch with just what it can mean to live the interim time more faithfully, both as individuals and as the body of Christ.

Participants and Leadership

Any number of groups can participate in the Bible study series. The entire congregation might be involved in a regular series, or smaller, more task-oriented groups, such as the church council, vestry, elders, deacons, or an interim steering committee, might work through the study.

The leadership can also come from a variety of sources because the goal of the study is to gain collective wisdom from the experience, rather than to impart knowledge from an expert.

Use

Here again, the possibilities are limitless and depend upon the needs and the creativity of the group. Each study will need approximately one hour and can easily be expanded according to the needs of the group. The Bible study can be used as a series, in stages, throughout the entire span of the interim period, or perhaps only occasionally when a particular issue or need arises. The material can also be shaped into a retreat design or used for a congregational meeting.

Organization of the Material: Impact, Percolation, and Reorganization

The Bible study resource is comprised of three major parts, despite the fact that the Christian community's experience is not so easily framed. Each part provides a choice of two scriptures. Both scriptures could be used if more time is available. The first part, "Who and Where We Were," invites participants to delve into the initial *impact* of the pastor's departure. Leaders and members will be using Psalm 107:1-9 and/or John 5:1-17 and will also benefit from reading chapters 2 and 6 of this book.

"Who and Where We Are Now," the second portion of the Bible study, suggests that a *percolation* is taking place in the congregation. Such percolation occurs as members begin to name the church's present identity in light of both its history and the in-breaking future. This section will use 1 Corinthians 1:10-17, 26-31 and/or Jeremiah 1:4-10. The dynamics are discussed in chapters 3,4,7, 8, and 9.

The last section provides a means to *reorganize* understanding as members begin to hear God's call to be the church in newly perceived ways. The congregation is beginning a commitment to new directions in ministry, described in chapter 10. There is also overlap with previous chapters, especially 7 and 8. Scriptures to be used are Luke 17:11-19 and/or Matthew 10:5-14.

Practical Suggestions

Some practical suggestions can benefit the facilitator and participants. If the facilitator keeps track of the unfolding discussion, then it will become easier to review progress, to correct for accurate understanding of discussions, and to be sensitive to feelings and contributions that might otherwise have been overlooked. A volunteer might take notes, or the facilitator could note down words and phrases to expand later.

Ask participants to bring their own Bibles to all sessions. In session 2, option B, they will also need to bring pictures of themselves.

It can be useful for the group to establish at the beginning of the series some simple ways of listening and speaking that will allow for a wide range of opinion within a respectful environment. These ground rules will become important when strong feelings emerge.

This study's approach to the biblical passages allows for personal identification with biblical characters and events. It also encourages playfulness in imagination. The subject matter may be serious indeed, but approaching it with a sense of fun and play can result in a deeper appreciation of the material.

Finally, participants will benefit most if they take the necessary time to explore, become involved, appreciate, and deepen relationships with each other, with the texts, and with God, who surely is present.

Part 1: Who and Where We Were

This Bible study relates to the interim church's first task, coming to terms with history. Experiences evoked in this study could include:

- Naming the issues
- Letting go of the fear of abandonment
- Affirming that healing is needed
- Celebrating and describing our history
- Finding ways to forgiveness

Before the Session Begins

- Review the key passage for the option you select and relevant portions of the book.
- Survey the group's meeting room, providing enough space for flexible seating.
- Provide the following for both options:

- a small table with visual focus to symbolize the Bible study's work, such as a lighted candle, flowers, or an open Bible
- study questions (found in the box), either posted or duplicated for small groups
- newsprint and markers
- bulletin board or flip chart and masking tape for posting reports
- paper or notebooks and pencils
- extra Bibles

- Particular resources needed for either option A or B:
  Option A: Duplicates of the cinquain instructions found in the box
  Option B: Chairs arranged in a semicircle

Option A: Discovering Our Hunger

Key Passage: Psalm 107:1-9

Introducing the Session

- Gather the group and offer an opening prayer.
- Explain that the participants will focus on Psalm 107:1-9 using solitary reflection, triads, and whole-group sharing.
- Divide members into groups of six and ask them to sit together.
- Have instructions ready for writing a cinquain.
- Ask each group to select an informal leader.

Bible Study

- Begin by having the passage read out loud to the entire group, asking the reader to use a normal reading pace. Then ask someone else to read the passage more slowly.
- Ask participants to sit in silence for five to ten minutes within each group and, individually at first, reflect about the passage using the following questions as focus:

What would be our experience as a church of wandering in the
    desert at this time?
For what do we presently hunger and thirst?
For what are we grateful?
For what are we sorry?
What do we hope to gain?
What does that city (verse 7) look like to you?
What, finally, is the heart of the matter for you personally?

- Now ask the participants in the small groups to write a simple poem using the cinquain poetry form, which consists of five lines and usually follows guidelines as in the boxed example below.
- Give them newsprint and markers, and either post the instructions for writing a cinquain or provide copies of the guidelines.

Cinquain Form: A Poem in Five Lines	Example
1 Title (a noun, one word)	Church
2 Describes the title (two words)	God's People
3 Action words or phrases about the title (three words)	Changing Seeking Wondering
4 Describes a feeling about title (four words)	Uncertain Hopeful Anxious Loving
5 Refers to title (one word)	Interim

- Gather all the participants together and share the poems. Discuss perceptions arising out of the poems. The leader may want to list these perceptions on newsprint under these columns:

What we hear	What we notice	What we need
about the church	about our feelings	to ask from God

- Close with a prayer asking God for help, and then pray the Lord's Prayer together.

Option B: Discovering Barriers to Healing

Key Passage: John 5:1-17

Introducing the Session

- Gather the group and offer a prayer for a sense of trust and the gift of discernment.
- Explain that the session will focus on John 5:1-17.
- Ask for volunteers to read these four parts: the narrator, Jesus, the paralytic, and the Jewish leaders.

Bible Study

- Ask the four volunteers to read the passage.
- Divide the whole group into four small groups and give them each a copy of the following boxed questions to ponder:

The Narrator Group
How do you think an outsider would see our church at this
time?
How do we see ourselves and our role as a church?

The Jesus Group
What do you see as the potential for health in this church?
How would Jesus' method for healing apply to our church?

The Paralytic Group
What is paralysis?
In what ways do we as a church feel paralyzed at this time?
For how long have we been paralyzed?
In what ways do we feel accustomed to, or comfortable in,
our paralysis?

The Jewish Leaders Group
In what ways do we want to keep the church the same and/
or play by the same rules?
Of what do we have a hard time letting go?

- Ask each group to summarize and list on newsprint insights gained from exploring that group's perspective. Post these lists.
- Ask the entire group to share their insights about this process.
- Close with a prayer of thanksgiving that might incorporate some of these insights.

Part 2: Who and Where We Are Now

This Bible study relates to three of the interim church's tasks—discovering a new identity, managing shifts in leadership, and renewing denominational linkages. Experiential components could include:

- Discerning our own gifts, liabilities, and unrealized potential as persons and as a church called to ministry
- Beginning to envision (in-breaking of the future)
- Naming conflict and brokenness
- Moving through "ordinary time," daily church life

Before the Session Begins

- Review the key passage for the option you select and relevant portions of the book.
- If you choose Option B, then be sure that participants were reminded to bring with them pictures of themselves and a journal.
- Survey the meeting room and put into place a flip chart, bulletin board, or blank wall for posting reports, and provide movable chairs.
- Provide the following materials for both options:
  - A small table with a visual focus, including a symbol representing the session's work
  - Extra pencils, paper, newsprint
  - Extra Bibles
- Particular resources needed for either option A or B:

  Option A: A large piece of newsprint or poster board with a very large circle drawn upon it, and several smaller cut-out circles for eventual inclusion within the larger circle

  Option B: A gong, bell, or another instrument as a way to symbolize call (just as the church bell calls worshippers to worship)

  Tables arranged so that subgroups may form

  Felt-tip markers, index cards

  Extra notebooks for journal entries

  Copies of the boxed Bible study questions

Option A: Becoming the Body of Christ

Key Passage: 1 Corinthians 1:10-17, 26-31

Introducing the Session

- Begin with an opening prayer, mentioning the church as a whole and its particular members.
- Give an overview of this session's plans, explaining that the focus will be a passage from Paul's letter to the Corinthians.

Bible Study

- Read 1 Corinthians 1:10-17, 26-31 to the group.
- Give people time to read this passage again by themselves.
- Ask participants to name the perceived ministries of your congrega-
  tion as you list them on newsprint (for example, the caregivers, the
  fund-raisers, the spiritual life group, the children's and youth minis-
  tries).
- Divide into subgroups representing those ministries, allowing parti-
  cipants to join the subgroups with which they most identify. Ask the
  subgroups to sit together to do the following tasks:
  - Name their group.
  - Write each group's name on a smaller circle.
  - Place the smaller circles within the very large circle previously
    drawn on the newsprint or poster board.
- Ask the subgroups to identify what it is that they want the church to
  know about their group's perspective during this interim time:
  - What is working in this area?
  - What is not working?
  - What does our group offer?
  - What needs improvement?
- Gather the group and list each group's perspective under its chosen
  name in the circle.
- Offer a prayer for guidance to find ways that these smaller groups
  can discover even greater unity as the one Body of Christ.
- Continue in the group as a whole and discuss the following:
  - What are the most puzzling aspects about this congregation
    today for which you would want to ask the apostle Paul for
    help?
  - What is the difference between "loyalty" and "following"?
  - Does loyalty relate to our discipleship in Christ?
  - In what areas have we demonstrated weaknesses that now
    could become a source of "good news" power?
  - How might our weaknesses be transformed into our call to
    ministry at this time in the life of the church?
- Remain together and write a letter to the apostle Paul in which you
  ask for help. Substitute the issues of your church for those in the
  Corinthian passage. (Perhaps this letter could be addressed, in some

form, to the entire congregation and presented during worship, in a newsletter, or on the bulletin board.)
- Close by reading 1 Corinthians 12:12 and inviting participants to pray the Lord's Prayer together.

Option B: What Is Our Call?

Key Passage: Jeremiah 1:4-10

Introducing the Session

- As participants enter, invite each one to sit around a table.
- Ask each participant to place his or her own picture on the table so that the participant is looking at it.
- When all are seated, ring the bell or play a chord on another instrument, asking for silence until the last vibration is heard.
- Give an overview of this session's plans, explaining that the focus will be Jeremiah 1:4-10. Have someone read the passage aloud to the entire group while everyone follows along in their own Bibles.

Bible Study

1. Solitude
- Ask participants to look at their pictures and sit quietly with the words, "Behold, I have formed you in the womb and I have put my words in your mouth."
- Ask them to consider the following questions, in quiet and alone, in relation to the Bible passage. (Offer adequate time, perhaps 10 to 15 minutes. They may want to use their journals.)

What does this mean to you for your call?
What does this mean to you for the interim period?
What personal gifts and strengths do you contribute to this in-
   terim period?
What areas of weakness might you name, and do they give you
   pause?
How do you respond to the content of the prophet's word to God's
   people?

2. Directed Conversation
- Group members may now share their responses with another person
  at the table, while turning their own pictures toward the person with
  whom they are speaking. (Allow two to five minutes for each
  speaker.)
- Ask that the listener listen without comment, perhaps jotting down
  pertinent points on index cards as they hear their partner's words.
- Ring the bell to reverse the role from speaker to listener.

3. Discussion and Feedback
- Provide time for participants to describe what they have discovered.
- Invite them to bring forward their index cards and pictures of each
  other and post them on the board. (The facilitator may wish to take
  a few moments to arrange the cards and pictures in clusters representing patterns such as ecumenical dialogue, hands-on mission,
  youth ministry, pastoral care. As the discussion progresses, the
  clusters of cards and photos may need to be changed.)
- Use the following questions to move the discussion forward:

What patterns do you see on the board?
What do these patterns have to do with our "call"?
What is it that we could be doing during this interim to become
    more attuned to God's call?
In what ways can the interim pastor be of help toward hearing
    God's call?
What does our church need to hear from our interim pastor?
In what ways do we want to keep the status quo? In what ways
    do we need to change?

- Close with a group-created chant, which would go like this: Each person reads aloud to themselves Jeremiah 1:4-10 at the pace and volume which feels right to them, gradually becoming aware of the sound and rhythm of others as they read, speak, and listen at the same time. In this manner, the group will build toward a chant.

Part 3: Who We Can Become and Where We Can Go

This portion relates to the last task of the interim church, commitment to new directions in ministry. Experiences evoked here may include:

- Feeling gratitude and receiving grace
- Becoming disciples and being accountable
- Becoming committed to a new life

Before the Session Begins

- Review the key passage you select and the relevant portions of the book.
- Arrange the room for the anticipated size of your group allowing for seating in both small and large groups (option A) or plan for comfortable seating and subdued lighting (option B).
- Provide the following materials for both options:
  - small table with a symbol to represent the session's work

- paper, pencils
- Bibles
- Particular resources needed for either option A or B:
  Option A: Post the incomplete sentences and copy the boxed Team
      Instructions found in the Bible study section.
  Option B: Flip chart and markers, or bulletin board and newsprint
      Copies of the boxed questions in the Bible study
      A basket, papers, and pencils for the closing

Option A: Becoming Committed

Key Passage: Luke 17:11-19

Introducing the Session

- Give the group a preview of the session plans.

Bible Study

- Ask the group to listen to the Bible story as it is read aloud.
- Guide the participants to spend five to ten minutes individually
  exploring the passage, asking people to linger on each word, testing
  its impact on the heart and mind, and perhaps underlining one or
  two words which carry the most impact.
- Now suggest that members jot down their responses to the passage,
  completing one or more of the following sentences:
      The heart of the matter is . . .
      To me this passage means . . .
      This passage perplexes me because . . .
- Divide the group into three teams for a dialogue time during which
  they will act out together:
      The Lepers
      The Jesus Team
      The Bystanders
- Ask each team to consider the questions listed below for a few

moments, then ask the first two groups to engage in a dialogue as they offer their own perspectives about the good of the church. During this conversation, the Bystanders group listens and observes. Continue the dialogue until it seems to you that the conversation has been concluded before hearing from the Bystanders.

Team Instructions

The Lepers: Think about the issues of your church in terms of its present needs for healing and growth and preparation for new pastoral leadership.
For what are you thankful as a church?

The Jesus Team: Think about the ways in which this church could be healed.
How might this church move forward?

The Bystanders: Make a summary about the insights you have received about:
Personal relationships to the church
The future of the church
Commitments which need to happen
Accountability of members

• Hold a discussion involving the entire group in order to help them discern priorities for the congregation's continuing work. Jot these down on index cards to be seen by the entire church, or write an article for the bulletin and/or monthly calendar, or share them during a moment of concern in worship.

Option B: Discerning Discipleship

Key Passage: Matthew 10:5-14

Introducing the Session

• Explain that you will be guiding the group in a meditation.
• Take some time for the group to settle down and be together in silence.
• Direct the individuals to close their eyes and give themselves over to their imaginations. Ask them to adopt a comfortable posture so that the scene will come to life for them as participants in it.
• Pray, asking God to coach the group and the individuals through the passage.
• Read the passage slowly as a group, with one or several sharing in the reading.
• Repeat the reading slowly.

Bible Study

1. Meditation/Visualization
• Imagine that you are sitting alone on a hill. What is the season? What are the colors around you? The weather? The sounds? The smells?
• You look down from where you are sitting and notice a group forming below you. One in the group begins to talk to the others. You sit very still, hoping that you will not be noticed. As you begin to listen to what is being said, you realize that it is Jesus talking to this group. As you listen and look more intently, you begin to recognize some of the people below. They are members of the congregation!
    Whom do you recognize?
    Why do you suppose they are there?
• You listen carefully. Jesus is commissioning these disciples, and he says something to them about what they are called to do as a church in this interim time.
    What does Jesus say?
    What are your reactions to his words?
    What are your feelings as you survey the scene?
• As you continue to look down, you realize that Jesus has stopped talking. He has turned around and he is looking up at you. He smiles, and even from this distance you can see much compassion

in his eyes. And then, he begins to walk up the path towards you.

What are your feelings as he approaches you?

Do you stand and walk towards him or do you sit and wait where you are?

- Finally, the two of you are face to face. He smiles and reaches out his hand. Before he has a chance to say anything, you blurt out that you have heard what he has said to the others and tell him what you think your role is as a disciple at this time in the life of your church.

What do you say to him?

What does Jesus say in response?

- You begin to feel comfortable talking with Jesus, enough to share with him the emotions you are feeling about the arrival of a new pastor.

What are the emotions you share with him? Reluctance? Eagerness? Fear?

Do you desire to pray with him for guidance?

- Jesus is fully there listening to you, standing before you. He is looking at you, lovingly and humbly. See him looking at you as he has taken in your words. And then he responds once again. He asks you what you need to let go of so that the movement towards the future can happen.

What dust do you need to shake off from your feet?

What do you say in response?

- He receives what you say and tells you that, in the telling, you have shaken off the dust. He blesses you and turns to walk down the path once again. You remain where you are for awhile, sitting quietly to take in all that has just happened. And then, you get up and walk towards the future.

2. Discussion and Conversation

- Divide the group into dyads and ask them to share with one another:

What was this experience like for you?

What did you discover about yourself?

What did you discover about what it means to be commissioned as disciples?

What do you need from others?

What do you want to give to others?

How will you express your commitment?

What did you discover about the mission for the church at this
time?

How do we prepare for new pastoral leadership?

What can be your personal role in all of this?

- Regather the group. Ask them to share their discoveries, making a
  list on newsprint.
- Invite each person to write down one commitment and place it in a
  basket in the center of the group.
- Close with prayer over these newly commissioned disciples.

Additional Passages for Study

The following passages may be useful for those who wish to develop
their own studies about the interim journey. They are selected and arranged with the tasks of the interim journey in mind, but leaders who
work with these passages may find that they evoke many different interim experiences.

Coming to Terms with History

Genesis 29:31-35	Leah is fruitful despite her circumstance.
Exodus 2:1-10	Miriam and the midwives save Moses.
Numbers 11:1-17	Moses complains to God in the wilderness and appoints elders.
Joshua 24	Joshua and the people renew their covenant with God.
2 Kings 22:14-20	Huldah the prophetess is consulted.
Psalm 13	The psalmist calls for help and expresses trust in God.
Isaiah 43:1-7, 18-21	God assures the people: " . . . the waters will not overwhelm you."
Mark 2:1-12	Friends carry a paralyzed man to Jesus
Mark 8:27-39	Jesus asks, "Who do people say that I am?" and offers his first prediction of the Passion.

Mark 10:17-31	Jesus offers a choice to the rich young man.
John 14:23-27	Jesus tells his disciples good-bye: "The Advocate will teach you . . ."
Acts 27	The ship is wrecked, but no life is lost.

Discovering a New Identity

Genesis 18:1-15	Sarah laughs when she hears that she will bear a child.
Genesis 29:31-35	Leah is fruitful despite her circumstance.
Genesis 32:22-32	Jacob wrestles with a stranger and says, "I will not let you go unless you bless me. . . ."
Deuteronomy 30:11-20	God speaks: "This commandment . . . is not too far away from you . . . choose life."
1 Samuel 1:9-18	Hannah waits patiently and finally births a son.
Nehemiah 8:1-3, 9-18	The exiles return, hear the law, and renew their covenant.
Psalms 30, 103, and 116	There is a joy in healing and recovery.
Ezekiel 36:22-36	God says, "I will give you a new heart and a new spirit."
Luke 14:15-24	The master commands his slave to bring dinner guests from the streets so that his house will be full.
John 9	The man born blind receives his sight.
John 21:4-19	Peter, who had denied Jesus, hears the command to "Feed my sheep."
Romans 8:18-30	"The whole creation stands on tiptoe. . . ."

Managing Shifts in Leadership

Exodus 6:1-13, 28-30	God calls Moses, who resists.
1 Samuel 17:38-49	David discards Saul's armor and chooses five smooth stones to slay Goliath.
2 Kings 2:1-3	Elisha receives Elijah's mantle.
2 Kings 5:1-14	Naaman the Syrian seeks healing in Israel.

Matthew 9:14-17	Fresh wineskins are needed for new wine.
Matthew 18:15-22	Disciples hold one another accountable and also forgive.
Matthew 20:1-16	Those laborers in the vineyard who are last are paid equally.
Mark 9:38-41	Jesus responds to the disciples who ask about "someone casting out demons in your name . . ."
John 11:1-12-18	Martha gives the representative confession of Christ.
John 15:1-4	"I am the true vine. . . ."
Acts 10:34-48	The Gentiles receive the Spirit.

Renewing Denominational Linkages

Matthew 25:14-30	Three servants receive varying talents.
Acts 3	Peter says to the beggar, "I have no silver or gold, but what I have I give you, in the name of Jesus Christ, . . . walk."
1 Corinthians 12	Many members are one in the One Body.
2 Corinthians 9	Paul exhorts Corinthians to generosity for their fellow Christians.

Commitment to New Directions in Ministry

Deuteronomy 31:4-8	Joshua is ordained as the next leader.
Deuteronomy 34	Moses sees the promised land but stays behind.
Psalm 126	"When the Lord restored the fortunes of Zion . . ."
Mark 7:24-30	The Syrophoenician woman confronts Jesus.
Mark 8:1-10	The disciples feed the four thousand.
Luke 14:25-34	"Which one of you desiring to build a tower does not sit down and count the cost?"
Luke 19:11-27	The parable of the talents.
John 1:29-34	John the Baptist points to the Christ as greater than he.
John 20:1-18	Mary meets the resurrected Christ in the garden.
2 Corinthians 4:1-18	Paul writes, "Therefore since it is by God's mercy that we are engaged in this ministry . . ."

Engaging the Developmental Tasks

R. Neil Chafin

Suggestions and Guidelines for the Interim Congregation

The following resource is an adaptation of material gathered from many interim ministry specialists by R. Neil Chafin, a member of the Interim Ministry Network and of its training faculty. A condensed version of a section in the Basic Education Manual of the Interim Ministry Network entitled "A Toolbox for the Developmental Tasks" is offered here as a resource for the lay leaders of interim congregations who are responsible for furthering the interim process. Chafin's permission to include this condensed version of his work in this book includes the following advice:

> Interim ministry will not succeed effectively if we take a cookbook approach to this work. Each congregation is different, with its own gifts, styles, and traditions. Interim ministry activities must fit the congregation and its traditions and norms. Many congregations are very capable of designing their own creative approaches and activities to engage large numbers of members in the developmental tasks. This Toolbox is presented only to prime the pump of creativity as congregational leaders look for ways to involve members in the interim process and its developmental tasks. It is important to be aware that the tasks do not always come in a neat order. I strongly believe we have to deal with "history" first, and that "commitment to new leadership" will always come last. In between, however, the needs of a particular congregation might require changing the order of the tasks. For example, congregations that have experienced power and control issues might need to work on "leadership and power shifts" before "new identity" can really be dealt with.

Again, in denominations where theological polarization is occurring, I have discovered that working on "rethinking denominational
linkage" is really a prerequisite to a new vision or "new identity."
Frequently, work on a later task will uncover some unfinished business on an earlier task.

This resource has a section for each of the developmental tasks, with
five subsections:

A The major issues contained in the task
B. Suggestions for engaging the issues by the congregation
C. Signs that the task has not been resolved or has not progressed
D. Indications that the task has been resolved or that substantial
    progress has been made
E. Additional resources relevant to understanding and furthering
    the task

1. Coming to Terms with History

A. Issues
*   Putting the tenure of former pastors in perspective
*   Acknowledging the past and accepting both the good and the bad
*   Deciding what is important and worthwhile to carry into the future
*   Appropriately ventilating feelings, grieving, accepting, and moving
    on

B. Suggestions
*   Tell the church's story, make a timeline for the church, update
    written history
*   Identify and celebrate watersheds in the congregation's life, signi-
    ficant moments, and accomplishments
*   Teach the grief process and provide for safe ventilation of feelings
*   Hold small-group meetings to reminisce and ventilate feelings
*   List strengths and weaknesses of previous pastor(s)
*   Listen and teach listening skills
*   Review covenants or statements which bind members together
*   Update files, records, and resource and member lists
*   Maintain healthy traditions while questioning problem ones

C. Symptoms of Non-Resolution
*   Continuing to dwell on the past
*   Being stuck in grief, anger, denial, guilt, alienation
*   Declining membership, giving, participation
*   Unwillingness to consider the "why" of traditions
*   Ghosts(s) of previous pastor(s) blocking openness to new and different leadership
*   Trying to clone the previous pastor or find his or her exact opposite

D. Indications of Resolution
*   Living in the present while accepting the past
*   Movement through the grief process; closure of relationship to previous pastor
*   Stabilizing membership, giving, participation
*   Open to change and ready to try new ideas
*   Asking process questions: Where are we going? What do we do now?
*   Investment in current and future issues; new mission statement
*   Healthy humor

E. Resources
Bridges, William. *Transitions: Making Sense of Life's Changes.* Reading, Mass.: Addison-Wesley Publishing Co., 1980.

Friedman, Edwin H. *Generation to Generation: Family Process in Church and Synagogue.* New York: Guilford Press, 1986.

"Healing Congregational Corporate Pain." (Training by LEAD Consulting, P.O. Box 32026, Raleigh, N.C. 27622)

Mead, Loren B. *Critical Moment of Ministry: A Change of Pastors.* Washington, D.C.: The Alban Institute, 1986.

Phillips, William B. *Pastoral Transitions: From Endings to New Beginnings.* Washington, D.C.: The Alban Institute, 1985.

Steinke, Peter L. *How Your Church Family Works: Understanding Congregations as Emotional Systems.* Washington, D.C..: The Alban Institute, 1993.

White, Edward A. *Saying Goodbye: A Time of Growth for Congregations and Pastors.* Washington, D.C.: The Alban Institute, 1990.

2. Discovering a New Identity

A. Issues
* Determining whether or not the congregation's image of itself is realistic
* Seeing the interim time as an opportunity for renewal and growth
* Congregation sees itself as an entity without a pastor; separating the church's identity from the former pastor's personality and style

B. Suggestions
* Work for ongoing reality testing
* Conduct congregational self-study to gain accurate information
* Hold cottage meetings to talk about what we are like and what we want to become
* Conduct study of neighborhood ministry needs
* Encourage program and resource assessments
* Develop a broad vision of congregation's future; establish goals and objectives

C. Symptoms of Non-Resolution
* Focus continues to be on the past
* Resistance to doing self-study
* Emphasis on blaming or on what's wrong; negative criticizing
* Low trust level, lack of authentic sharing
* Identity confusion: Who are we?
* Leaders and others continue to consult the previous pastor
* Maintain same old programs, even when they don't fit present needs
* Rush through the interim

D. Indication of Resolution
* Focus on present or future
* Willingness to do self-assessment
* Congregation faces reality; affirms its true identity

- Growing excitement about the congregation's envisioned future
- What happens next? How can we help?
- Spirit of inclusiveness and outreach
- Rising trust level, humor, and patience with the search process

E. Resources

Ammerman, Nancy T.; Jackson W. Carroll; Carl S. Dudley; and William McKinney. *Studying Congregations: A New Handbook* (a revision of the *Handbook for Congregational Studies*). Nashville: Abingdon Press, 1998.

Center for Social and Religious Research (surveys), Hartford Seminary.

Oswald, Roy M. and Speed B. Leas. *The Inviting Church: A Study of New Member Assimilation*. 1987. Reprint. Washington, D.C.: The Alban Institute, 1993.

Schaller, Lyle E. *Looking in the Mirror: Self-Appraisal in the Local Church*. Nashville: Abingdon Press, 1984.

3. Leadership Changes during an Interim

A. Issues
- Power and control of decisions and direction of congregation
- Healthy, realistic, and open decision making; wide ownership of decisions
- Managing conflicts to promote congregational unity
- Honoring past leaders and finding ways to keep them involved
- Burn-out and drop-out of leaders; leadership development

B. Suggestions
- Assess leadership needed to reach interim goals and recruit leaders to meet those needs
- Affirm leaders' different styles and talents; use Myers-Briggs Type Indicator or other tools
- Teach conflict management and resolution skills
- Rethink process of developing leadership and lengths of terms of office; write position descriptions

- Recognize and celebrate the leaders who are going out of office
- Determine whether or not decision-making processes are congruent with those stated in governing documents
- Open the decision-making process to all members; seek input, share information widely

C. Symptoms of Non-Resolution
- Divisions, destructive sub-grouping, competition, avoidance
- Power plays; making end runs around process
- Win-lose decisions
- Decisions aren't clear, aren't carried out, or fall apart
- Search committee becomes a power center and does not communicate with membership
- Secret meetings, self-authorized decisions, gossip, and rumors
- Exclusiveness, blaming, avoidance of conflict

D. Indications of Resolution
- Open leadership and decision-making structures
- Interdependency; readiness to work together; volunteers come forward
- Win-win decisions
- Clear decisions with follow-through
- Shared leadership in maintenance and developmental tasks
- Election, acceptance, and support of new leadership
- Both old and new leaders involved
- Inclusiveness: Conflicts and differences are dealt with openly

E. Resources
Halverstadt, Hugh F. *Managing Church Conflict*. Louisville, Ky.: Westminster/John Knox, 1992.

Johnson, Barry. *Polarity Management: Identifying and Managing Unsolvable Problems*. Amherst, Mass.: Human Resources Development Press, 1997.

Leas, Speed B. *Moving Your Church Through Conflict*. Washington, D.C.: The Alban Institute, 1985.

Oates, Wayne E. *The Care of Troublesome People*. Bethesda, Md.: The Alban Institute, 1994.

Saarinen, Martin F. *Life Cycle of a Congregation*. Washington, D.C.:
The Alban Institute, 1985.

4. Renewing Denominational Linkages

A. Issues
*   Healthy partnership with the denomination
*   Authority, dependency, interdependency, counter-dependency
*   Congregation's tendency to see judicatory or denomination through
    former pastor's eyes
*   History of the relationship, dollars, and trust; shared mission

B. Suggestions
*   Make use of denominational resources: staff, programs, facilities,
    literature, training, retreats
*   Encourage denomination to give clear information about its expec-
    tations, requirements, resources, and programs
*   Identify common interests of church and denomination
*   Identify and affirm church members who hold denominational
    positions
*   Allow for ventilation of feelings about denomination
*   Have denominational ministries and programs lifted up in newslet-
    ters or during mission moments in worship

C. Symptoms of Non-Resolution
*   Resistance to denominational requests or suggestions
*   Criticism of denominational personnel and programs
*   Failure to meet pledges and budgets
*   "We-they" outlook

D. Indications of Resolution
*   Willingness to accept help and resources
*   Appreciation for the denomination's traditions and missions
*   Denomination's resources and facilities are used
*   Stable or increased giving to denomination: dollars and people

E.   Resources
National, denominational resources such as curriculum, mission information, and the like.

Walrath, Douglas Alan. *Frameworks: Patterns for Living and Believing
Today.* Cleveland: Pilgrim Press, 1987.

5. Commitment to New Directions in Ministry

A.   Issues
- Wide ownership of and excitement about the shared vision for the
  future
- Getting a good match between the pastor and the congregation
- Clear and shared expectations between clergy and congregation
- Clean exit of interim pastor and consultant; good closure of the
  interim period

B.   Suggestions
- Planning for the start-up period with the new pastor
- Bring good closure to interim
- Interim sharing insight with incoming pastor
- Ministers-in-transition support programs such as a Pastoral Rela-
  tions Committee
- Making sure transition rituals are in place
- Exit interview with interim and denominational representative

C.   Symptoms of Non-Resolution
- Anxiety and rushing the search process
- Trying to hire the interim as the permanent pastor
- Unrealistic or unclear expectations of the new pastor
- Inability to agree on choice of pastor
- Low energy level, lack of humor
- Failure to issue a call; discouragement with search process

D.   Indications of Resolution
- Focus on the future
- Enthusiastic preparations for new pastor (housing, installation,
  start-up)

- Clarity and consensus on leadership style desired of new pastor
- Increasing levels of involvement and ownership in process
- Appreciation of interim process and leaders
- Willingness to say goodbye to interim
- Evident energy and healthy humor

E.   Resources

Oswald, Roy M. *New Beginnings: A Pastorate Start-up Workbook.* Washington, D.C.: The Alban Institute, 1989.

———. *Pastor as Newcomer.* Washington, D.C.: The Alban Institute, 1977.

Resources for Congregational Self-Study and Planning

(Adapted from materials widely shared by interim leaders of several denominations)

Congregations in the interim time will want to consult their denominational leaders about procedures and materials for self-study and planning which have been developed for use by churches of their tradition. In addition to denominational resources, congregations have found the following sources for surveys, study materials, and services to be helpful:

1. The Alban Institute, 7315 Wisconsin Avenue, Suite 1250W, Bethesda, MD 20814-3211.
    Consulting services for church planning, conflict resolution, and other needs.
2. Hartford Seminary Center for Social and Religious Research, 77 Sherman Street, Hartford, CT 06105.
    Church Planning Inventory, Pastoral Search Inventory, and Parish Profile Inventory, plus collation and interpretation services.
3. Church Planning Services, 3555 Hillside Court, Hoffman Estates, IL 60195.
    Church-planning survey form designed to gather information from members regarding demographics, beliefs, and values, as well as their priorities, feelings, and perceptions about the church. Congregation may add questions pertinent to their purposes. Assistance with collation and interpretation is also available.
4. Percept, 151 Kalmus Drive, Costa Mesa, CA 92626.
    Demographic information and detailed profiles of specific geographic locales, based on postal zip codes. Saves the time and expense involved in gathering basic sociological data for your

neighborhood or parish. Transparencies facilitate study and interpretation of data.

5. Search Institute, Thresher Square West, 700 South Third Street, Suite 210, Minneapolis, MN 55415-1138 (800-888-7828)."*Voices of Faith: A Portrait of Congregational Life"* *survey form to be filled out with assistance in interpretation of data.*

What Is the Interim Ministry Network?

Growing out of congregational studies done by Loren Mead and Roy Oswald of the Alban Institute, the Interim Ministry Network was organized in 1980 and incorporated in 1981. A non-profit, religious organization, the Network is an international and ecumenical association of almost 1,500 interim ministry specialists, consultants, and church leaders. Some 25 denominations are represented in this organization committed to "serving the church during times of transition."

The Interim Ministry Network provides education and skill development for interim pastors and lay and denominational leaders to help congregations understand and make the most of the opportunity presented when there is a change of pastors. Believing the interim period to be a prime time for renewing congregations and other organizations within the Body of Christ, the Network provides special resources for interim specialists, consultants, and lay and denominational leaders:

> Education and information on the interim process
> Professional support systems
> Education and professional development
> Standards for the practice of interim ministry

For more information and a listing of their resources, including helpful videos and printed materials, contact the Interim Ministry Network, 5740 Executive Drive, Suite 220, Baltimore, MD 21228. Telephone 410-719-0777. Fax 410-719-0795.

Developing an Interim Ministry Covenant or Contract

(Adapted from materials widely shared by interim leaders of several denominations)

1. Term of service: For how many months will the agreement be in effect?
2. Hours per week the interim is expected to be "on the job." Are regular office hours expected? If so, what is the guideline?
3. Examples of pastoral services to be provided by the interim:

   - Leadership in working on the interim process and furthering the five developmental tasks
   - Sunday and special worship services
   - Resourcing of committees and/or organizations
   - Counseling
   - Sacraments
   - Visitation of sick and shut-in, and providing care to the distressed
   - Special services such as weddings and funerals
   - Confirmation program and/or membership classes
   - Adult education
   - Administration of church office, staff, program
   - Denominational/ecumenical activities
   - Others

4. Relationships
   - To whom is the interim pastor responsible?
   - What kinds of reports from the interim pastor are expected, and to whom are they directed?
   - Will there be any interface with the new pastor in the start-up period?

- Will there be a pastoral relations committee or personnel committee for the interim pastor?
- What are the interim's responsibilities to and for the rest of the church staff? Paid staff? Volunteers?
- How does the church view the relationship of the interim pastor to the denominational staff members, particularly that person assisting with the search process?

Note: The covenant/contract should include (1) a statement that the interim pastor agrees that she or he will in no way influence the congregation or its officers in matters relating to the search for and call to the new pastor, and (2) a statement that the interim pastor will not be a candidate for the permanent pastorate.

5. Congregational responsibilities during the interim period:
   - Further the five developmental tasks of the interim period
   - Self-study
   - Regular attendance in worship
   - Continued financial support to the church and its mission and ministries
   - Sustained lay leadership
   - Engagement in a goal-setting process
   - Prepare for the calling of a full-time, resident pastor

6. Clergy compensation:
   - Honor denominational guidelines for pastoral support, recognizing that the interim time is not a time to cut back clergy support
   - Cash salary of $_____ per month
   - Annuity, health plan, and family protection plan for the interim pastor
   - Travel expenses of $_____ per month or _____ cents per mile, including travel to and from the church and church functions
   - Housing allowance (if parsonage is not to be used), including utilities and phone, except personal, long-distance calls
   - Vacation pay accumulating at two days per month of service, or _____ weeks if interim ministry is in excess of 12 months
   - Continuing education provisions of time and funds

"It is agreed that this covenant/contract shall be terminated upon (30, 60, 90) days' notice by either the interim pastor or by the official board of the church or it shall be renewable by the mutual consent of the interim and the official board, and that 30 days' notice shall be given by either party of intentions to exercise or decline such renewal. It is further agreed that the interim shall under no circumstances be a candidate for the position of resident pastor."

Because of the importance of a designated denominational staff person remaining closely in touch with the church and the interim pastor during the interim period, it is strongly suggested that that person or the appropriate official from the denomination be a party to the signing of the covenant/contract.

Why Should the Interim Pastor Not Be a Candidate for the Permanent Call?

The following is listed as the rationale for not considering the interim pastor/transition specialist as a candidate for the permanent position:

1. An interim pastor/transition specialist has an advantage over other possible candidates who may desire to be considered for the position because he or she has more visibility to the congregation. This makes it unfair to others who may be interested in the position, but who will not have the same visibility.

2. An interim pastor/transition specialist will always have a following, but also almost always will have those who are not favorably committed to him or her. If he or she were to be called to be the pastor, there would be built-in opposition from the very beginning.

3. If the decision is made to consider the interim pastor/transition specialist along with the others being considered and the interim pastor/transition specialist does not get the position, there could be hurt feelings that would jeopardize the remainder of his or her interim work until the pastor is called.

4. A precedent could be set which would result in pastors seeking interim positions with the specific idea of putting themselves in a better position to be considered and called as the pastor, thus greatly damaging the whole call process.

5. The congregation itself may pass up better leadership than it is getting, even with a good interim pastor/transition specialist, if it fails to consider a larger number of potential pastoral candidates.

6. Interim ministry is unique and an interim pastor/transition specialist may often lead in ways that would be acceptable as an

interim pastor/transition specialist, but would not be acceptable to some in the congregation were he or she to remain as the pastor.

7. Other pastors will know of the ministerial ethics involved and will know that those have been broken if an interim pastor/transition specialist is called. The result could be a lack of fellowship and broken relationships with other pastors.

8. During the time of interim, the congregation often is uniquely vulnerable and therefore develops a relationship based on need and insecurity. While this can be useful in leading a congregation to prepare for the incoming pastor, it could make for a very inappropriately skewed decision for a permanent call.

Used by permission of the Interim Ministry Network, Baltimore, Maryland.

Litanies of Welcome and Farewell to the Interim Pastor

Litany of Welcome
For the Beginning of the Interim Journey

A church family is constantly changing. Loved ones come to the end of their lives. Individuals come and go in our church life. It is important and right that we recognize these times of passage, of endings and beginnings. Today we share the time of welcome with Pastor _____ whose time as our interim pastor/transition specialist begins.

Leader: Pastor_____, in the presence of this congregation will you commit yourself to this new trust and responsibility, and promise to discharge your duties in harmony with the constitutions of the church?

Pastor: *I will, and I ask God to help me.*

Leader: Will you love, serve and pray for these people of God, nourishing them with the Word and Holy Sacraments and lead them forward during this important time of change?

Pastor: *I will, and I ask God to help me.*

Leader: Will you lead this people of God in giving faithful witness to the word and making known the love of God through loving service among themselves and in this community?

Pastor: *I will, and I ask God to help me.*

Leader: Almighty God, who has given you the will to do these things, give you the power of his Spirit so that you may perform them with strength and compassion.

Congregation:	Amen.
Leader:	I ask all of you, now, people of this congregation, will you receive this messenger of Christ, Pastor _____, who continues the work of bringing the Gospel of hope and salvation? Will you regard him/her as a fellow servant of Christ and work with him/her in the ministry of this congregation?
Congregation:	We will.
Leader:	Will you pray for him/her and honor him/her for his/her work's sake and in all things strive to live together in the peace and unity of Christ?
Congregation:	We will.
Leader:	By your statements of commitment and the affirmation of this congregation, we welcome you as interim pastor/ transition specialist of this congregation in the name of the Father and of the Son and of the Holy Spirit. Amen.

Litany of Farewell
For the End of the Interim Journey

Leader:	A church family is constantly changing. Loved ones come to the end of their lives. Individuals and families come and go in our church life. It is important and right that we recognize these times of passage, of endings and beginnings. Today we say farewell to Pastor _____, whose time as our interim pastor has come to an end.
Pastor:	*I thank _____ Church, its members and friends, for the love, kindness, and support shown me these last _____ months. I thank you for accepting my leadership. I recall with joy the many things we have been able to accomplish together and with sadness the things we were not able to do. I ask your understanding and forgiveness for the mistakes I made and for the times I let you down.*
Congregation:	We receive your thankfulness, and we offer our forgiveness for any failures. We accept that you now leave us to minister elsewhere. Your influence on us will not

	leave us, even though you depart from us. We express gratitude for your time among us and ask your forgiveness for our shortcomings and sometimes flagging faith.
Pastor:	*I forgive you your failures and accept your gratitude, trusting that our time together and our parting are pleasing to the Christ we are called to serve.*
Leader:	Do you, the members and friends of _____ Church, now release Pastor _____ from the duties of interim pastor?
Congregation:	We do, with the help of God.
Leader:	Do you, Pastor _____, release _____ Church from turning to you and depending on you?
Pastor:	*I do, with the help of God.*
Leader:	Do you offer your encouragement for the continued ministry here at _____ Church?
Pastor:	*I do, with the help of God.*
Leader:	Let us pray.
Congregation:	God, whose everlasting love for all is trustworthy, help each of us to trust the future, which rests in your care. During our time together, we have experienced laughter and tears, hopes and disappointments. Guide us as we carry these cherished memories with us in new directions until the time when we are completely one with you and one another. In the name of Jesus Christ, we pray. Amen.
Leader:	Go, now, Pastor _____, surrounded by our love and led by the promises of God, the presence of Jesus Christ, and the guidance of the Holy Spirit. Amen.

*Litanies of Welcome and Farewell are used by permission of the
Interim Ministry Network, Baltimore, Maryland.*

Form for the Evaluation of the Interim Pastor

(Adapted from evaluation materials widely shared by interim leaders of several denominations)

Interim ministry specialists are continually seeking to improve their skills in assisting congregations through transition. A denominational colleague will share your observations and suggestions with your interim pastor for the purpose of helping her or him to grow as a professional. The evaluation is not a "grading" procedure, but an open and honest sharing of reflections. Please use this form to record your responses and return it to your church moderator, president, or warden.

Your Name _____*(optional)*

Your Position in the Congregation_____

In which of the following do you usually participate?
_____ weekly worship
_____ adult education
_____ committee work
_____ occasional volunteer activities
_____ other _____
(be as specific as you like)

Your Contact with the Interim Pastor

On average, other than weekly worship, how often did you have contact with the interim pastor?
_____ two to three times a week (or more)
_____ once a week
_____ two to three times a month
_____ once a month
_____ other_____*(please specify)*

Please give your evaluation by circling one of the numbers on the rating scale for each of the following:

1.   How clear was the interim pastor in interpreting to the leadership of the church the purpose and tasks of the interim period?

    1   2   3   4   5
(unclear)   (clear)

Give examples of how your interim pastor accomplished the above.

2.   How well did the interim pastor help the church fulfill those tasks?

    1   2   3   4   5
(very poorly)   (very well)

3.   How well did the interim pastor deal with situations of conflict?

1   2   3   4   5
(very poorly)   (very well)

4.   How well did the interim pastor relate to other members of the
      church staff?

1   2   3   4   5
(very poorly)   (very well)

5.   Rate the interim pastor's performance in the following:

a. Preaching and conduct of worship

1   2   3   4   5
(poor)   (excellent)

b. Pastoral oversight

1   2   3   4   5
(poor)   (excellent)

c. Administration (work with boards and committees)

1   2   3   4   5
(poor)   (excellent)

6.   What would you have liked more (or less) of from the interim
      pastor?

7.   Sum up, in your own words, what you feel was the impact of the interim ministry on the life of the church.

8.   This is what I have learned about a church during the interim period.

Form for the Evaluation of the Interim Process

(Adapted from evaluation materials widely shared by interim leaders of several denominations)

Church _____

Interim Pastor _____

Date _____

When evaluating the interim process, it is helpful to keep in mind that the developmental tasks are the work of the congregation, and the management of the overall process is the responsibility of the interim leader. It is important to consider how the congregation has been involved in furthering the interim agenda, as well as how well the process was managed.

Rating Scale: 1. Not done at all

2. Partially done/done, but not well

3. Adequately done

4. More than adequate/we learned things that will help us in the future

5. Exceeded my wildest expectations

Your Name _____(optional)

Your Position in the Congregation _____

In which of the following do you usually participate?
_____weekly worship
_____adult education
_____committee work
_____occasional volunteer activities
_____other _____(be as specific as you like)

Your Contact with the Interim Pastor

On average, other than weekly worship, how often did you have contact
with the interim pastor?
_____two to three times a week (or more)
_____once a week
_____two to three times a month
_____once a month
_____other_____ (please specify)

When asked to provide a rating number in the following items, use the
Rating Scale at the beginning of this section.

1. Coming to terms with history: acting on the realization that the
former pastor has departed; that the relationship can never be the same
again; and that a new relationship will be accepted
    a. Rating number _____
    b. What can you point to as evidence that the task was done?
    c. What did the interim pastor do to help?
    d. What else could the interim pastor have done to help accom-
        plish this task?

2. Establishing an identity: claiming a new awareness of self that is
    independent of the previous pastor
    a. Rating number _____
    b. What can you point to as evidence that the task was done?

   c.   What did the interim pastor do to help?

   d.   What else could the interim pastor have done to help accomplish this task?

3.   Shifts in power: constructively allowing alternative or new congregational leadership to come to the fore

   a.   Rating number _____

   b.   What can you point to as evidence that the task was done?

   c.   What did the interim pastor do to help?

   d.   What else could the interim pastor have done to help accomplish this task?

4.   Rethinking denominational ties: seeing the denomination as a potential resource and support rather than as an adversary

   a.   Rating number _____

   b.   What can you point to as evidence that the task was done?

   c.   What did the interim pastor do to help?

   d.   What else could the interim pastor have done to help accomplish this task?

5.   Commitment to new leadership: wholeheartedly supporting the newly called pastor

   a.   Rating number _____

   b.   What can you point to as evidence that the task was done?

   c.   What did the interim pastor do to help?

   d.   What else could the interim pastor have done to help accomplish this task?

6.   What is your overall feeling about the interim ministry period?

7. What additional comments do you want to make?

NOTES

Introduction
1. Tony Campolo, *Can Mainline Denominations Make a Comeback?* (Valley Forge, Pa.: Judson Press, 1995).
2. Loren B. Mead, *The Once and Future Church* (Washington, D.C.: The Alban Institute, 1991).
3. Andrew Rook, "Changes," *Take Notice: The Newsletter of Dore and Totley United Reformed Church of Sheffield, England.* Vol. 55/3 (March 1998): 1.
4. Loren B. Mead, *Critical Moment of Ministry: A Change of Pastors* (Washington, D.C.: The Alban Institute, 1986).
5. The Interim Ministry Network, Inc., P.O. Box 21251, Baltimore, MD 21228.

Chapter 2
1. From a reprint of an article attributed to Loren B. Mead and entitled "Clues About Pastoral Care of People and Congregations."
2. Ibid.

Chapter 3
1. David Bohm, *Wholeness and the Implicate Order* (London: Ark Publishing, 1980), p. 196.

Chapter 4
1. Peter M. Senge, *The Fifth Discipline: The Art and Practice of the Learning Organization* (New York: Doubleday/Currency, 1990), p. 240.
2. Ibid., p. 241.

Chapter 5

1. Loren B. Mead, *New Hope for Congregations* (New York: Seabury Press, 1972).

2. This phrase is from Ray Welles, *Between the No Longer and the Not Yet* (St. Louis: Office for Church Life and Leadership, United Church of Christ, 1977).

3. William A. Yon, *Prime Time for Renewal.* 1974. Reprint. Washington, D.C.: The Alban Institute, 1977.

Chapter 6

1. James Lane Allen, *The Mettle of the Pasture* (New York: MacMillan and Co., 1903), pp. 161-162.

Chapter 7

1. American Baptist Personnel Services (1-800-ABC-3USA, ext. 2446) provides a questionnaire (ABPS-3) that congregations can use. Of course, you can develop your own brief questionnaire asking whatever seems important for you to know about yourselves from this "outside-but-in" vantage point.

2. I have been indebted through the years to the insights of Frederick Buechner for this way of thinking about vocation. He sets it forth first in *Wishful Thinking: A Theological ABC* (New York: Harper & Row, 1973).

3. Contact the national office of your denomination for such services. Information related to such topics as race, ethnicity, age, and gender for a desired geographical area can probably be obtained from that office. Large businesses in your community might also have demographic information available through their marketing departments. Keep in mind that this kind of information cannot answer all your questions. In fact, you might discover that you have even more questions after you examine the data. Compare and contrast what you read with your own observations.

4. One of the best resources for this is produced by the Baptist General Conference and is entitled "Leadership Planning: Alive in Christ, Transforming Communities and Changing the World," written by John C. Dickau, copyright 1994. Order through: BGC, 2002 South Arlington Heights Road, Arlington Heights, IL 60005-4913.

5. My staff colleague, Bob Shoesmith, shared this and other ideas related to getting a sense of the needs of your neighborhood.

6. My favorite print resource for engaging in a process of congregational gift discernment is "Discover Your Gifts and Learn How to Use Them," produced by CRC Publications, 2850 Kalamazoo Ave, SE, Grand Rapids, MI 49560 (1-800-333-8300). A leader's guide and student manual are provided. For a survey only, "How To Identify Your Spiritual Giftabilities" is a revised version of a tool created by Herb Miller. Pastors report that they have administered this during worship, adult class, or new-member orientation with effectiveness. Published in *Net Results* 16A (April 1995): 9-16 ($5.00). Call New Results in Texas: 1-806-762-8094. The original, and some say the black belt of gift surveys, first came out of Willow Creek Church.

7. There are many ways to undertake a more in-depth self-study of your congregation. Your denominational office may be able to recommend one that seems right for your congregation. American Baptist Churches of Connecticut has used "New Song," which undertakes a study of the congregation from a systems perspective with an eye to planning for renewal. This process is adapted from a doctor-of-ministry project by Bob Shoesmith and is entitled "Congregational Systems." The Parsons/Leas resource listed in the bibliography is also a highly recommended tool for community analysis.

Chapter 10

1. David Odum, "One Year Later: The Effectiveness of Intentional Interim Ministry," *The Journal of the Interim Ministry Network* 2, no. 1 (February 1998): 33.

2. Loren B. Mead, *Critical Moment in Ministry: A Change Of Pastors* (Washington, D.C.: The Alban Institute, 1986), p. 32.

3. Ibid., p. 49.

Tool 1

1. Robert C. Worley, *Dry Bones Breathe* (Elgin, Ill.: Brethren Press, 1978), p. 69.

BIBLIOGRAPHY

(Sections 1 through 5 are based on a bibliography developed for the Interim Ministry Network by Susan DeSimone. Section 6 is a list of additional resources contributed by the authors of this book.)

Section 1: Interim Ministry Theory and Practice

Ammerman, Nancy T.; Jackson W. Carroll; Carl S. Dudley; and William McKinney. *Studying Congregations* (a revision of the *Handbook for Congregational Studies*). Nashville: Abingdon Press, 1998. Guidance in analyzing your congregation, including ready-to-use survey forms.

Anderson, Leith. *A Church for the 21st Century*. Minneapolis: Bethany House, 1992.

Bridges, William. *Managing Transitions*. Reading, Mass.: Addison-Wesley Publishing Co., 1993.

Campolo, Tony. *Can Mainline Denominations Make a Comeback?* Valley Forge, Pa.: Judson Press, 1995.

Easum, William. *Dancing with Dinosaurs*. Nashville: Abingdon Press, 1993.

Macy, Ralph. *The Interim Pastor*. Washington, D.C.: The Alban Institute, 1978.

Mead, Loren B. *Critical Moment of Ministry: A Change of Pastors*. Washington, D.C.: The Alban Institute, 1986.

_____. *The Once and Future Church*. Washington, D.C.: The Alban Institute, 1993.

Narowitz, Cathleen R. *Worship Resources for the Interim Time*. Valley Forge, Pa.: American Baptist Church, 1991.

Phillips, William B. *Pastoral Transitions: From Endings to New Beginnings*. Washington, D.C.: The Alban Institute, 1988.

Porcher, Philip. *What You Can Expect from an Interim Pastor and an Interim Consultant*. Washington, D.C.: The Alban Institute, 1980.

White, Edward A. *Saying Goodbye: A Time of Growth for Congregations and Pastors*. Washington, D.C.: The Alban Institute, 1990.

Wuthnow, Robert. "Responding To A New Generation of Seekers." *Congregations: The Alban Journal*. Washington, D.C., March/April 1986.

Zuck, Nevin H. "Ten Marks of a Church Alive . . . and Healthy." The Andrews Center, Elgin, Ill. (Spring 1996).

Section 2: Denominational Guidelines

Davis, James. *Interim Pastoral Ministry,* Lutheran Church, Baltimore, Md.: Interim Ministry Network, 1988.

Gripe, Alan G. *Interim Pastors Manual*, Presbyterian Church USA, Philadelphia: Geneva Press, 1997.

Interim Ministries: An Overview for Church Leaders (Book 1). The Church Deployment Board of the Episcopal Church, 815 Second Ave., New York, NY 10017-4594.

Interim Ministries: Practical Helps in Interim Ministry Management (Book 2). The Church Deployment Board of the Episcopal Church, 815 Second Ave., New York, NY 10017-4594.

Interim Ministry Guidelines and Resources for Local Churches, Rhode Island Conference, United Church of Christ, 56 Walcott St., Pawtucket, RI 02860, 1994.

Leaders Guide for a Local Church Workshop on the Developmental Tasks. Valley Forge, Pa.: American Baptist Church, 1993.

Odum, David L. "One Year Later: The Effectiveness of Intentional Interim Ministry." *The Journal of the Interim Ministry Network* 2 (February 1998): 33. (Odum is Director of the Center for Congregational Health, Division of Pastoral Care, North Carolina Baptist Hospitals, Inc., Medical Center Blvd., Winston-Salem, NC 27157-1098.)

Section 3: Systems Theory and Congregations

Bohm, David. *Wholeness and the Implicate Order*. Fort Washington,
    Pa.: Ark Publishing, 1980.
Capra, Fritjof. *The Web of Life: A New Scientific Understanding of
    Living Systems*. New York: Anchor/Doubleday: 1996.
Fortel, Deborah G., and David R. Sawyer. "A Family Systems Approach
    to Building Healthy Relationships across Our Denomination."
    Church and Society Periodical, Presbyterian Church (Sept.-Oct.
    1990): 47.
Friedman, Edwin H. *Generation to Generation: Family Process in
    Church and Synagogue*. New York: Guilford Press, 1985.
Hopewell, James, F. *Congregation: Stories and Structures*. Minneapo-
    lis: Fortress Press, 1987.
Mitchell, Kenneth R. *Multiple Staff Ministries*. Philadelphia:
    Westminster, 1988.
Senge, Peter M. *The Fifth Discipline: The Art and Practice of the
    Learning Organization*. New York: Doubleday/Currency, 1990.
Steinke, Peter L. *Healthy Congregations: A Systems Approach*.
    Bethesda, Md.: The Alban Institute, 1996.
_____. *How Your Church Family Works: Understanding Congrega-
    tions As Emotional Systems*. Washington, D.C.: The Alban Insti-
    tute, 1993.
Wheatley, Margaret J. *Leadership and the New Science: Learning
    about Organization from an Orderly Universe*. San Francisco:
    Berrett-Kohler, 1992.

Section 4: Conflict and Its Management

Baruch Bush, Robert A., and Joseph P. Folger. *The Promise of Media-
    tion*. San Francisco: Jossey-Bass, 1994.
Halverstadt, Hugh. *Managing Church Conflict*. Louisville, Ky.:
    Westminster John Knox Press, 1991.
Heifetz, Robert A. *Leadership without Easy Answers*. Cambridge,
    Mass.: The Belknap Press, 1994.
Johnson, Barry. *Polarity Management: Identifying and Managing Un-
    solvable Problems*. Amherst, Mass.: Human Resources Development
    Press, 1992.

Leas, Speed B. *A Lay Person's Guide to Conflict Management.*
Washington, D.C.: The Alban Institute, 1979.

Leas, Speed B., and Paul Kittlaus. *Church Fights: Managing Conflict in the Local Church.* Philadelphia: Westminster, 1977.

Section 5: Leadership in the Interim Church

Callahan, Kennon L. *Effective Church Leadership.* San Francisco: Harper, 1990.

Dale, Robert D. *Good New from Great Leaders.* Washington, D.C.: The Alban Institute, 1992.

DePree, Max. *Leadership Is an Art.* New York: Dell, 1989.

Gilbert, Roberta M. *Extraordinary Relationships.* Minneapolis: Chronimed Publishing Inc., 1992.

Olsen, Charles M. *Transforming Church Boards.* Bethesda, Md.: The Alban Institute, 1995.

Rendle, Gilbert R. *Leading Change in the Congregation: Spiritual and Organizational Tools for Leaders.* Bethesda, Md.: The Alban Institute, 1998.

Richardson, Ronald W. *Creating a Healthier Church.* Minneapolis: Fortress Press, 1996.

Roberts, Wess. *Leadership Secrets of Attila the Hun.* New York: Warner Books, 1985.

Sawyer, David. *Work of the Church: Getting the Job Done on Boards and Committees.* Valley Forge, Pa.: Judson Press, 1987.

Stevens, R. Paul, and Phil Collins. *The Equipping Pastor.* Washington, D.C.: The Alban Institute, 1993.

Section 6: Additional Resources
(contributed by the authors of this book)

Craig, Robert H., and Robert C. Worley. *Dry Bones Live: Helping Congregations Discover New Life.* Louisville, Ky.: Westminster John Knox Press, 1978.

Easum, William. *How To Reach Baby Boomers.* Nashville: Abingdon Press, 1991.

Friedman, Edwin H. *Friedman's Fables*. New York: Guilford Press, 1990.

Marshall, Frank, and Carole Hatcher. *Church Visioning Workbook*. Bethesda, Md.: The Alban Institute, 1997.

Mead, Loren B. *The Developmental Tasks of a Congregation in Search of a Pastor*. 1977. Reprint. Washington, D.C.: The Alban Institute, 1980. (Now contained in Mead's book, *Critical Moment of Ministry*.)

_____. *Transforming Congregations for the Future*. Bethesda, Md.: The Alban Institute, 1994.

Oswald, Roy M., and Robert E. Friedrich. *Discerning Your Congregation's Future: A Strategic and Spiritual Approach*. Bethesda, Md.: The Alban Institute, 1996.

Parsons, George, and Speed B. Leas. *Understanding Your Congregation as a System*. Washington, D.C.: The Alban Institute, 1993.

Steinke, Peter L. *How Your Church Family Works*. Washington, D.C.: The Alban Institute, 1993.

Woods, C. Jeff. *Congregational Megatrends*. Bethesda, Md.: The Alban Institute, 1996.

Yon, William A. *Prime Time for Renewal*. 1974 Reprint. Washington, D.C.: The Alban Institute, 1977.

CONTRIBUTORS

Bonnie Bardot. Bardot received her M.Div. from Yale Divinity School. She served as an installed pastor for five years and since 1987 has been an interim minister in the Connecticut Conference of the United Church of Christ.

Andrew E. Carlsson. Carlsson, a pastor of the Evangelical Lutheran Church in America, has served congregations in western Pennsylvania since 1962 and has been an intentional interim pastor since 1988. Through his Seed Sower Ministries, he presents workshops and training for congregational lay leaders and pastors. He is a member of the Interim Ministry Network faculty.

R. Neil Chafin. Chafin is the president of CareNet, Inc., the Outpatient Counseling Network of North Carolina Baptist Hospitals in Winston-Salem, North Carolina. He is a member of the Interim Ministry Network and serves on its educational faculty.

Terry E. Foland. A senior consultant with the Alban Institute and an ordained minister of the Christian Church (Disciples of Christ), Foland has worked with interim ministry for nearly 30 years. He was on the steering committee that launched the Interim Ministry Network and served as a member of the IMN board for 12 years. Foland also helped shape interim ministry support programs for two regions of his denomination. He lives in Harrisburg, Missouri.

Thomas A. Hughart. Hughart is a Presbyterian minister with a doctorate in ethics from San Francisco Theological Seminary. A trained interim pastor, he has served First Presbyterian Church in Greenwich,

Connecticut, and Central Presbyterian Church in New York City. His home base is Bedford, New York.

Robert W. Johnson. Johnson is an intentional interim minister in the United Church of Canada. He serves as an interim specialist in the Toronto, Ontario, region. An active member of the Interim Ministry Network, he has been a faculty member for training interim pastors.

Janet Parsons Mackey. During the past 12 years, Mackey has served as an interim minister in both congregational and denominational United Church of Christ settings. Before those experiences, she served in several settled positions. Mackey lives in Natick, Massachusetts, and especially values the home base provided by her neighbors, family, and friends.

Nancy Miller. Prior to attending seminary, Miller worked in the insurance industry. Since her ordination as an Episcopal priest, she has been a college chaplain and currently serves as the deployment officer for the Episcopal Diocese of Connecticut. She is married to the Rev. Barry Miller, a trained interim specialist and human resources consultant. They live in Hartford, Connecticut.

Barbara W. Miner. A wife and the mother of two college-age daughters, Miner is a United Church of Christ minister who has served as interim minister for congregations. She is the Massachusetts Conference's program minister for a conference/retreat center committed to the renewal of the church through the personal growth, education, and spiritual nourishment of its members.

Roger S. Nicholson. Following a 21-year settled pastorate, Nicholson served as intentional interim pastor for the Connecticut Conference of the United Church of Christ. After serving 20 congregations in 15 years as an interim specialist, he retired in 1996. He still serves as a training coordinator for the Interim Ministry Network.

Philip G. Porcher. An Episcopal priest, Porcher has served for over 40 years in congregations in South Carolina and Virginia and recently retired after 20 years as director of vocation ministry for the Diocese of Southern Virginia. He was one of the cofounders of the interim ministry training program developed by the Alban Institute and later helped establish the Interim Ministry Network. He has been training and working with interim pastors and consultants since 1976.

David R. Sawyer. Sawyer has promoted, taught, and practiced interim ministry, although he is currently pastor of Spirit of Life Presbyterian Church, a new church development in suburban Minneapolis. He has a Ph.D. in organizational communication from Ohio University and is the author of *Work of the Church: Getting the Job Done on Boards and Committees* (Judson Press).

Warren Schulz. Schulz has been an interim pastor with the Evangelical Lutheran Church in America since 1977 and has served more than 25 congregations. He was on the steering committee that gave birth to the Interim Ministry Network and served as the network's first president. He lives in St. Paul, Minnesota.

Linda Lea Snyder. Snyder experiences God's newness through the identities of woman, mother, feminist, pastor, and interim specialist. She currently serves as associate executive minister for the American Baptist Church of Connecticut.

Paul N. Svingen. Called by the Minneapolis Area Synod of the Evangelical Lutheran Church in America, Svingen has served 20 interim pastorates. A member of the Interim Ministry Network since 1984, he has served the network as president, board member, and faculty coordinator, and now serves as program director. His 1990 D.Min. thesis for Luther Seminary in St. Paul, Minnesota, is entitled "Intentional Interim Ministry with the Evangelical Lutheran Church in America."

Roger S. Nicholson is a United Church of Christ minister who recently retired after a 15-year career as an intentional interim pastor. He served the Connecticut Conference of the United Church of Christ as minister-at-large, guiding more than 20 congregations through pastoral transitions. Prior to becoming an interim ministry specialist, he served as senior pastor of the South Congregational Church in East Hartford, Connecticut for 22 years. A graduate of Tufts University and Yale Divinity School, he received a Doctor of Ministry degree from Hartford Seminary in 1983. He took his basic training for intentional interim ministry under the Mid-Atlantic Association for Training and Consultation in 1982. An active member of the Interim Ministry Network, he is a member of its educational faculty, working as a coordinator of basic education events. He is also chairperson of the Network's Judicatory Liaison Committee.

"A time often approached with dread, the 'time between settled pastors' is portrayed by Roger Nicholson as a grace-filled opportunity for renewing life and leadership and purpose within a congregation. Primarily offered as a handbook for lay members of congregations, Temporary Shepherds *charts the course for the interim period from beginning to end and offers helpful questions But it will also enable those ministers about to leave or join a parish to fulfill their particular ministries at those crucial times with greater awareness and effectiveness. And the common wisdom and standards which emerge in the writing will bring clarity and consistency for denominational leaders who have such an important role with congregations during their 'interim times.' Solidly grounded in Scripture and theology, filled with references and tested resources,* Temporary Shepherds *is a welcome addition to the shared wisdom of the church."*

The Rt. Rev. Andrew D. Smith
Bishop Suffragan of the Diocese of Connecticut
(Episcopal)
Hartford, Connecticut

Made in the USA
Las Vegas, NV
11 February 2022